A CEREBELLUM SOCIETY PUBLICATION

CEREBELLUM LITERARY SOCIETY
Volume I

WINDS OF TIME

Editors
Emma Feix Alberts
Lydia Crompton
Michele Fishman
Sharon L. Konschak
Judith A. Lambert

a cerebellum book

A Cerebellum Book

Published By:
Cerebellum Publications

This work comprises fiction. Names, places, characters and incidents are either products of the authors' imaginations or used fictitiously. Any resemblance to actual events or locales or persons, living or dead, is entirely coincidental.

The Cerebellum Literary Society
PO Box, 1204 Absecon, N.J. 08201

Cover Design and photo by Lydia Crompton
Editor's Photograph by Drew S. Fishman

First Edition 2002

Copyright © 2002. All rights reserved. No part of this book may be reproduced or transmitted in any form or by any means, electronic or mechanical, including photocopying, recording, or otherwise, or stored in or introduced into a retrieval system, without prior written permission of the respective, individual authors featured here, excerpts in a review. Published by permission of the authors featured.

Publisher's Cataloging-in-Publication

Winds of Time: a collection of Poetry & Prose-1st ed.
P.cm.
Library of Congress Control Number: 2002093495
ISBN: 0-9722341-0-1

1.American literature-21st century
I.Alberts,Emma F. II.Crompton, Lydia III.Fishman, Michele
IV.Konschack, Sharon V. Lambert, Judith A.

PS   *********

QB*********

Printed in the United States by Morris Publishing
3212 East Highway 30
Kearney, NE 68847
1-800-650-7888

ACKNOWLEDGEMENTS

We are most grateful to the following people for their help in making this book a reality;

Stephen Dunn, Pulitzer Prize winning poet and Professor at Richard Stockton College for his contribution and support.

Bette Stephens of Bette's Fine Framing for all her help.

The Noyes Museum, Oceanville, New Jersey, for its involvement in the arts and their generosity in allowing the society to use their facilities.

Drew S. Fishman for the professional portrait of the society's editors.

A portion of the proceeds from the sales of this book will be donated toward *Breast Cancer Research.*

Cerebellum Society

The society is like the roots of a tree, emerging from different backgrounds, joining together to form the trunk, growing and branching out in all directions. The group's cohesiveness is the basis of the society's success in bringing about the publication's showcasing of talented writers. The board of directors is of one mind in their selections.

We at Cerebellum believe that all writers seek a new vision. We are proud to showcase these select few. We invite you to discover the landscapes that these talented writers have painted for you.

Table of Contents

BJ Ward	1
Sharon L. Konschak	6
Judith A. Lambert	14, 25
Lydia Crompton	21
Michele Fishman	34
Emma Feix Alberts	41
Yvonne Lambert	47, 102
Tammy Stewart	52
Michael Jemal	54
Sarah Mench	57
John Carothers	58, 93, 113
Gerri Black	65
Karen M. Peluso	67
Suzanne Koiro	70
PJ Tighe	72
Geoff Rosenberger	74

Susanne Kerrigan	84
Sean Toner	86
D.P. Williams	91
Robert E. McCarty	100
Tony Bataglia	108
Janet A. Feix	110
Marion W. Maguire	120
Editors' Choice	122
Forward, Stephen Dunn	123
R.J. Corradino	125

BJ Ward

The Poems I Regret In My First Book

Irretractable, obnoxious children
having tantrums on the dog-eared tabletops
of these pages, screaming out,
'Failure! Failure!'
in an otherwise classy joint.
Words I wrote so long ago
while drunk, perhaps, or worse, young ---
subversive little syllables that slipped
my editor's eyes, smuggled in, cloaked
by the good, rightly -legal stuff---
now conspiring to kill the whole book
with ugliness.
There they are --- irrevocable
in their deficiencies, the runts of the litter
making the most noise,
whom I can't punish by banishing
to the room 'Out of Print'
without sequestering the good children as
well.
(This is how books called Selected Poems are
born.)

So here I am, in front of an audience,
peddling a book which should be half
quarantined,
not reading certain pieces,
keeping those kids on the bench
while about nine players swing for the fence
and hopefully carry the team.

Sex With Emily Dickinson

"I couldn't help myself," I told my wife.
"I was reading her before I went to sleep,
and I can't control what I dream."
"What was it like?" she asked, wearily.
I started quoting Wild Nights, Wild Nights,
which she kept saying over and over---Emily,
that is---
in the dream, but I didn't mention
the moment of climax
when suddenly Emily turned into Helen
Vendler
and told me I was a bad poet.

My wife looked at me
as if my Penis were on trial---
usually the Inquisitor, it was now the
Defendant.
"That's okay," she finally smirked, "Zero
at the Bone. There's something I haven't told
you.
The first time I read your book,
I dreamt I was in a threesome
with Robert Bly and Robert Penn Warren.
We did it on a huge drum, men in suits
banging in unison around us."
she paused.
"It must have been a Robert thing,"
then: "I couldn't help myself."

We sat there a while, nothing arriving
and nothing leaving, our dreams
causing a caesura of sorts. I finally said,
"My sex, I'm sure, was more iambic than
yours."
"You should know," she rejoined,
"I always hated sex that felt formal."

And again we kissed right there, her lips
shaped like the light of a locomotive
at the dark end of a tunnel, which led to
touching
which felt like the rumbling of a waiting
platform,
which led to great sex, which arrived
like one of those extra trains
they run on holidays.

After it was over we lay there
between the mattress & covers---words on
opposite pages
finally closed in a book and touching,
which made us a sort of Braille upon each
other
there in the dark, in our magnificent bed---
reading the language that rose up from us all
night.
As soon as we were Written, we were Read

Aubade

I love how this morning the world spills
around my breakfast plate, the newspaper
opened beneath it---
Afghanistan's rebuilding next to my toast as
my mug rests atop the list of celebrity
birthdays.
Today's morning is large enough for Alfred
Hitchcock and Don Ho to have the same
birthday, both residents now on the continent
of my kitchen table.
The coffee machine warbles its symphony of
frogs and radiators as if to sing of the arrival
of the coffee itself.
The fried eggs start applauding.
Before I can stand, Victoria and her green
eyes float into the room and dock on the
shores of my table's new democracy, pouring
me a cup.
And I want to be as precise with my joy today
as all those poets are with their suffering.
I want to tell you how on August 13th I was
happy even as the world surrounded my
breakfast.

Now I see how Fidel Castro and Danny
Bonaduce also have this birthday and they
will be forever linked in my mind
with Hitchcock and Don Ho, and that's all
right, because this was the day the coffee and
the light and Victoria's sculptured neckline
were pieces of my life breaking open, and how
they conspired to make the world once more
bearable again and again and again.

Upon Being Told Again There Are No Rhymes For Certain Words

Crossing to my studio eighty yards
through some briars, I lug a verbal freight:
both volumes of the New Shorter Oxford
English Dictionary. I contemplate
a carpenter bringing a lumber pile
to his wood shop --- I want to build
structures
from words that readers could live in awhile.
I know it's rare, tricky stuff, such scripture -
scores of poets, still no rhymes for purple.
Bonds could beat McGuire and Ruth --- but
orange?
I'd reconstruct Heaven, or usurp Hell ---
write till I swing open like a door hinge.
I arrive --- a rogue who'd refurbish town.
I take my pen, begin to nail things down.

Sharon L. Konschak

Modern Art

Lupus comes clothed
angry
purple
sulfuric yellow

A phantom,
brace wrapped
round its leg
leans heavily
on the canadian crutch
ugly armband
metal covered with gray rubber
fettered like a shackle

It's what I call living art,
the prothesis in its cradle
like the shape of a child
in the sculpted
arms of its mother
so smooth I want to touch it
but when I do, it pricks

After viewing the painting, *Black Cross*, by
Georgia O'Keefe

Penance

I'm always restless when another slips
into my world of dreams

I toss, turn, then freeze

watch her story open wide
like a mouth that comforts children

point to moldy headstones
of people I never knew

and think,
she ought to have a cross...

The sun, a sour aspirin,
goes down in waves of ether
unmarked,
for woman leave no wake...

So now she has her crucifix
crude, rigid, nothing human in it

symbol of hope,
the priest declares, clearing his throat

I guess he thinks that dusk is just like dawn

I guess he forgot about the nails

This is how you should love me...

Like a brown bag lunch
tuna on rye
with crust

Like that 19 year old
hands outstretched
waiting to leave
marks of passion
on my back

Your lips, curl- cornered
to my thin
crooked grin
look of hunger
piercing like a hook

      This is how you should love me...
In a field of grass
your whole hot body's length
along my own
dissolving flesh
melting bone

Like it's the last night of the world
and we are two trees embracing,
when the wind blows
you can hear us
rub each other

We've just been baptized

in the cool font of lust
and we scream
in the doorway
of our beginning

        This is how you should love me...
In the breathless wedge
between night and dawn
you are quenched in my cold heart
I thaw in your core of fire
both magnetized by desire

As you take me
with such strength
and stretch me in between
the moon and the Chevrolet
that made me crave you so

Like you mean it
with all crust
stripped away

Word Play

I love to lick words the way I licked cherry
Tootsie pops my brother would swipe as a kid
from the corner store.

Love it when sagacious, assiduous, damask,
or my new word: verisimilitude,
tinge my tongue, thicken the spit at the start
of my throat, sweet

as those pops, red and slick with every lick
it took to make mini batons out of them:
sticky spheres I pitched straight up
with the haughtiness of a child
more often neglected than seen.

Abrupt, turgid, or knuckles, have jaw-
breaker flavors: there's caramel in mercurial,
salsa in hunk, and syncopation has aromas
of buttermilk and honey. Those tastes of

reparation still bittersweet today as I rotate,
curve and mold words in my mouth,
repeating syllables like acts of contrition,
then sticking out my new tongue--

tangy and saccharined-- to the obscurities of
meaning.

Midnight Craving

I'm hungry
and
want to break
all the rules

I mash potatoes
with heavy cream
drizzle them with gravy
steam my green beans
in chicken broth
and
ride straddled
to my lover
let our stomachs arch
break even
when his skin
tastes of lime dust
on muskmelon
and my lust
is all persimmon juice

Then when my fingers
slip up his hips again
in sacred syncope fervor,
he laughs and
I become dessert
let my hair messy itself
in his fingers
and pull the silence
in around us

cabbie

philadelphia row houses
are glued
dark
alleys drenched with cardboard
rain

chilly for the season
he says
i almost scream
out how
your voice was
is like your thighs
and lips
yes
yes

a fishmonger unloads
on canal street
rain bouncing off the sidewalk
hard
it seems to rain up
the window wipers
scratch
faster and faster
every thump
squeak
thump
squeak

at the airport
the sky cap yanks
the door
open
what's your destination he says
i toss him
a five
my bag is heavy
and torn

Judith A. Lambert

Without Cause

There are six of us living in this small three bedroom council house on the main street in Cookstown, Northern Ireland. It's my Mum and Da, two sisters, my brother Terry and myself. Terry is the oldest, nearly five years my senior. He's a fine figure of a man, well over six feet tall with a broad chest and massive shoulders. In spite of his size, he's gentle and kind, never finding fault with anyone. He's always looking for the good side of a person, even when there is none. With his black curly hair and blue eyes, Mum says if he'd been born in America, he'd have been a film star.

I'm sure you know, this part of Ireland is occupied by the English. Cookstown has the distinction of being one of the first towns to have a fully functioning electronic surveillance installation in operation 24 hours a day. With their equipment, the soldiers can zero in on conversations from the enclosed telephone call box in front of our house. A half-mile up the road from us is the military barracks that house the British troops for all of Armagh, Belfast, and Derry. The barbed-wire topped brick wall that encloses the barracks is four stories high.

Cookstown used to be a huge market town. Every Saturday, farmers from all over brought their produce and livestock to the open square marketplace. The town was filled with the sound of deals being made and men and women laughing and having a grand time. No more. Now there is a barbed-wire encircled checkpoint at either end of the town. No one enters or leaves without being questioned, and in many cases, cars and trucks are searched, and the contents thrown out on the roadway. The past ten years have been particularly violent. My mum keeps the front curtains closed so she doesn't have to look at the checkpoint, which is in the middle of the street directly across from our front door. When she leaves the house to go up to the chapel each morning, she keeps her head down and walks quickly up the hill.

In the midst of it all, my brother, Terry smiles and goes about his business avoiding the soldiers as much as possible. When they do stop him, Terry is polite and respectful. It would be foolhardy to be otherwise.

Terry is the best brother a fella could have. He lets me tag along whenever he goes to the shops and talks to me like one of the guys. He jokingly says, "We can't have you sitting around the house with the girls, now can we? They'd make a Nancy boy out of you."

In the evenings we usually go down to the sweet shop. The girl behind the counter, they call her Eileen, fancies Terry. And if the truth be told, he feels the same. While they talk and cut up, I walk around the shop trying to figure out how best to spend my meager allowance. Should I get the jaw-breakers that last a long time or the caramel creams that are two for a penny? Sometimes Eileen gives me bits and pieces of broken candy when no one's looking. Terry always buys licorice whips or colored mints to take home to Mum. She loves sweets but more than the candy, she loves that Terry remembers to bring her something.

It's coming on to Christmas and a big dance is being held in Armagh. Terry and his pals have been talking about it for weeks. They're after borrowing a car and are chipping in on the gas. There are great discussions around the kitchen table over what to wear, when to leave, and the best route to take. I love listening to Terry and his friends.

After a bit, Terry looks over at me, "So what do you think, Tom, should we take the back road and avoid the traffic?"

Feeling important I say, "Sure, it might be quicker, but what about the soldiers? Aren't they likely to be patrolling the back road, just looking to stop someone?"

Terry knows how fearful I am of the soldiers. We've all heard stories of innocent people being arrested, just for being in the wrong place at the wrong time.

"Right you are, no sense courting trouble."

Terry promised when I got older, I could go to the dances with them. Now, just being part of the planning was enough.

On the night of the dance, the five boys met at our house. My sister, Bridget, got out the camera and took their picture. They were laughing and joking, and posing for the camera. Even Da was enjoying the craic.

"Get out of here the lot of you and let me listen to my program." He joked.

After they left, Da and I listened to the wireless while Mum and the girls went up the road to a neighbor's house.

At 10 o'clock there was a banging on the door. It was Terry's pal, Sean. He looked a wreck; his clothes were dirty and he had a wild look in his eyes.

"Terry's been hurt," he gasped, "you'd better come to the hospital."

"Tom, run up the street and get Mum and the girls. I'll get Fr. Nolan to drive us."

When we got to the hospital there was a lot of confusion. People from the dance were sitting slumped over in the chairs. A few were sitting on the floor, leaning against the wall all waiting to be seen. Two girls were holding blood-soaked towels on various parts of their bodies. Terry was nowhere to be seen. Da and the priest asked the nurse at the front desk if they could see Terry. Maybe Sean made a mistake; maybe Terry wasn't hurt.

"He's in the operating room," the nurse said. "The doctor will speak with you when he's done."

Father Nolan led us to the chapel. It was dark and quiet. I knelt down and started to pray. It didn't make any sense for God to take Terry. He'd never done a mean thing in his life. Sure wouldn't he be of more use alive. I began to bargain with God. If he spared Terry, I would pay attention at Mass and not skip out after communion. I'd not complain about saying the Rosary, and I'd give the responses loud and clear, not in my usual mumbling way. It was almost midnight before anyone came to get us.

"He's still unconscious but you can go in for a few minutes," the doctor said.

Terry was lying on the bed with a bunch of tubes in him. He was as white as the sheet, but there wasn't a mark on him, that I could see. I couldn't believe it, the ones out in the waiting room were all cut up and bleeding, yet they had gone home. What was Terry still doing here?

"He has internal injuries and a blunt force trauma to the head. The first 24 hours will tell the story." The doctor said.

I wondered what the hell that meant. No one seemed to know what happened. One of the boys said they were walking into the dance and there was an explosion somewhere behind them. Metal, glass, and chunks of concrete just flew at them from all directions. Terry was closest to the explosion and took the worst of it in his back.

I stood there looking at him, thinking how much I loved him. He was always teasing me about being sensitive.

"Don't be sappy," he'd say, "be tough, be a man." I knew he was just trying to protect me, to mark my card, to let me know life was not easy.

Terry had always done well at school. There was even talk of a scholarship to the university, but he knew money was tight so when he got his leaving certificate, he got a job. There was never a word of what might have been.

Down at the Pub, Terry would listen to the old men tell the same stories over and over and pretend he was hearing them for the first time. He had a powerful voice and was the first one up on the floor when the singing started. He always had a kind word to say and when he had the money he stood the old fellas to a pint. You could tell he really liked people and people liked him.

He had a great sense of humor and if the joke was on him, he enjoyed it twice as much. One time his pals at the garage, where he worked, got these big bear paws that were part of a display and taped them on his back. He went all over town with those things stuck on him. You should have heard him laugh when he found out. "That's a good one, on me," he said.

The doctor suggested we go home and get some sleep but Da decided he would keep watch, just in case.

I woke Sunday morning thinking it was a bad dream. One look at Mum told me different.

"We'll go to early Mass and then to the hospital. Maybe there will be some news by then." She said.

The priest called for prayers for Terry from the altar. I somehow felt he would come out of it. He was strong and healthy, everyone said he lived a charmed life.

Da met us at the door as we entered the hospital. The grim set of his mouth and the red puffiness of his eyes told us it was not good. He could hardly control himself. I had never seen my father cry. I turned away and walked into Terry's room.

I looked at him lying there in the bed. His color was good. I thought that was a positive sign. Those bloody doctors, what did they know? All the tubes were gone and the sun was shining through the window. Terry loved the sun. He often said nothing could go wrong when the sun was shining.

All these thoughts running through my head strengthened my belief that Terry would be all right. He'd be home in no time and the joke would be on them, thinking a piece of flying metal that hardly made a mark could do him in. No way.

I touched Terry's hand, he looked like he was about to smile, like he had just heard a joke, or had the last laugh. Then he died.

Lydia Crompton

The Ancestral Home

"There are only two tragedies in life: one is not getting what one wants, and the other is getting it."   -Oscar Wilde

The house bustled
strangers and relatives crossed paths
an endless flow of scavengers
needful things taken
while I, an outsider, watched helpless
Its owner, my husband's grandfather,
planted in the family plot
free of material possessions

Greed cast over the crowd
calculating the resale before purchase
one by one
items displayed on the auction block
or tossed if broken
like the legless wooden watch box
erasing family memories

The hollow shell was last
vultures dove for the Victorian Mansion
two rivals vied for the deed
I watched in disbelief
with the legless box under my arm

The final price paid by Bob Smith Demolition

The Dusty Book

I scoured the land for that soul mate
lover, friend and companion
looking for the perfect inside and out
Only to have fruitless journeys
an unending list of one night dates

I had passed you a million times
without giving you a second look
You were held in regard by all,
for your wit, knowledge
and brilliant humor

I saw your gentleness
holding the hand of your
red-headed toddler daughter
Giving of yourself with time or money
from the heart, without reservation

Qualities I searched
for in a life companion

"Never judge a book by its cover"
though we do
I saw you as the dusty jacket of an old book
The quote echoed inside me
I surprised myself
by inviting this dusty jacket
out to dinner on a double date

Your stories captivated me
throughout dinner
Overwhelmed me when
you paid our table's check

On the dock, we watched the moon
reflect on the river
We hugged and kissed
for the first time.

I was drawn into your book
and discovered the novel
that was written
is the story of us

The last word

I heard there's no medical basis, dear
that it is totally unnecessary

But I know you lose feeling
if you don't remove it

Skin is skin
they take it from there
harm is done

That's because you are a woman
You will never understand

I understand perfectly
I like it the way it is

My rule as a new father
Do it the way, it has been done
for generations
Do it *now* before he has any memory.

Judith A. Lambert

The Reunion

The reunion information came in the mail along with a questionnaire. I couldn't believe after 40 years anyone cared what his high school classmates were doing. High school had been something to get through, to graduate and get out into the real world. I had skipped the twenty-fifth reunion and was inclined to do the same for this one. But curiosity got the best of me; maybe it was time to go back.

I called Carol, my best friend from high school. We had kind of drifted apart over the years but it never mattered how long it had been between phone calls, we are always able to pick up where we left off as if it were yesterday.

Skipping the usual formalities, I asked, "Are you going to the reunion?"

She was pretty quick with her answer. "No, I don't think so. Most of those people didn't speak to us when we saw them every day in school. What makes you think they'll talk to us now?"

"They might have changed. We have. Don't you want to see what everyone looks like?"

"I don't really care." She said.

It took me a good hour to talk her into just thinking about going. She still would not commit totally but a maybe was as good as a yes in my book. I couldn't explain, even to Carol, why I just had to see how the 'popular' people had fared. Were those voted most likely to succeed, successful? Did the guy with all the black curly hair go bald? Had the cheerleaders gotten fat?

My next phone call was to Barbara. She was in our class but had come to our school as a freshman while Carol and I had been friends forever. Barbara was an easy sell. She'd go anywhere for a party. Where Carol was less than enthusiastic, Barbara was jubilant.

"It'll be great. We'll see who ended up together. Do you think any of the cheerleaders married football players? Who was that girl with the long blond hair, I hope she got fat." Barbara pulled no punches; she was looking for some vindication.

As I looked through our yearbook I tried to remember some of the people we had been friendly with.

Looking at the prom pictures brought back a particularly awkward time in my life. My parents were very strict and did not allow me to date, so I was not even thinking about going. As it turned out, the school secretary, Miss Zimmerman, approached my parents and asked if I might be allowed to attend since I was on the prom committee and had done a lot of work decorating the gym.

Miss Zimmerman must have been very convincing because my parents agreed to let me go if I would be home by midnight. Talk about Cinderella. She then set about finding me a date. How in the world she decided on Richard, I have no idea. We looked like Mutt and Jeff together; but he was nice and polite and agreed to have me home before I turned into a pumpkin. Of course he had to come to the house before the prom and pass my father's inspection. As I waited in the kitchen my father gave him the third degree. I have no idea what was said but Dad was favorably impressed.

In looking through the yearbook, I came upon a picture of us at the prom. What memories that brought back. I had borrowed a dress that was at least two sizes too big. It was strapless, but Aunt Margaret, the family seamstress, remedied that. She fashioned a cape from a piece of netting, attached it to either side of the top of the dress with snaps and draped it across my chest and over my shoulders. When she finished it completely covered what little bit of cleavage I had.

The worst part of the prom picture was my hair. I have always had very straight hair, which I wore just hanging down or pulled back in a ponytail. My mother insisted that I have my hair curled for the prom and sent me around to Miss Irene's on Main Street. I think Miss Irenes' specialty was old ladies because the style she gave me definitely did not belong on a teenager. She set my hair in pin curls, sprayed it with some kind of lacquer, and sent me home with my head wrapped in a scarf to return the next day for the comb-out. When all the pins were taken out, she smeared a big glob of VO-5 on my hair and then styled it. In addition to having a mess of tight little curls all over my head, my hair was greasy-looking as well.

Even my father could not resist a comment. "You paid good money for that?"

The prom itself was a blur. The only proof that I actually went is a faded, out-of-focus picture, taken in front of Richard's car. My mother had saved it in an old shoe box. The official prom pictures I threw away right after the prom. The miracle of all this, I found out later, is that Richard has fond memories of the evening. Of course, he also thinks we dated for a while, and I am pretty sure my parents would not have bent the, "no dates until you're 18" rule. The prom was a one-time only exception. By the time I was 18, Richard was safely away at college.

A few nights later, I got a phone call from Richard. He had called one of the girls in charge of the reunion, to find out who was coming and to get my phone number.

Richard, who had always hated school, had become a teacher.

"You have to go," he said. "It'll be great. Remember John, the guy that always carried a briefcase? I always wondered what he had in there. If he comes, I'm going to ask him. Do you think Dottie will be there? You know I always had a crush on her."

"You and half the senior class."

"It will be nice to see everyone again. I hope some of the teachers come. So are you going?"

"As a matter of fact, Carol, Barbara and I are driving up together."

"Great, what are you wearing?"

"What are you, the fashion police?"

"No, I just want to be able to recognize you."

In the end we decided to e-mail each other pictures. As it got closer to the reunion date, I spoke a few times with Sharon, who was on the planning committee. She was on the color guard and had been part of the "in crowd" but she had always been friendly. As she gave me the lowdown on our classmates, I racked my brain trying to put names and faces together.

Ellen was one of the few people I remembered. She had been part of our so-called sorority. When we were growing up, Ellen had lived in an apartment over the barbershop on Main Street. We all thought that was very exciting. Ellen's mother was a widow and worked so the one and only time we played hooky, we went to Ellen's apartment. We sat around the living room with the curtains drawn in fear of being caught. No one even missed us as we had been sent out on job interviews that day and weren't expected to return to school. That was about as daring and adventurous as we got.

So now there were four of our group going to the reunion. Carol was still not sure but I finally talked her into it. I told her I was hoping to get some ideas for a story I was doing for the local newspaper on reunions. Carol agreed to go and help me take notes.

After many phone calls regarding clothes and transportation, the reunion day arrived.

I, who had protested, "I'll just dig something out of the closet" spent two hours trying on various outfits. I changed shoes at least four times. The weather was warm but it might turn cold. Should I wear a coat? I finally decided to take one, just in case. I had long ago cut my hair short so I spent over an hour with a curling iron and hair spray in an attempt to achieve that Meg Ryan tousled look. I didn't quite pull it off, but I was not going to chance going to the hairdresser again.

When I picked Carol up, she was a bundle of nerves, while I had to pretend to be calm. Luckily she didn't offer me anything to eat or drink or I would have thrown up on the spot.

We drove to Barbara's, who was even more enthusiastic than she had been on the phone. Carol and I had opted for the conservative, dressy look but Barbara had gone all out. She wore black satin pants, a leopard print top under a very hip-looking velvet jacket. She pulled it off beautifully. Barbara agreed to drive; mostly I think to show off her new car. We all piled in and were at last on the road to the reunion.

We made good time and arrived without mishap save for a few illegal u-turns at the very end. The reunion was held in a large hotel. I think quite a few people had stayed at the hotel the night before. I spotted Richard immediately pacing nervously in a little room off the lobby. I suddenly realized that we all felt the same. Forty years was a long time. None of us knew what to expect.

Everyone wore a nametag with their graduation picture on it. We were recognized at once, which might have been because the three of us were together, as we had always been in high school. Barbara has a very high-pitched, distinctive voice; some people, who didn't recognize her face, knew the voice. People came over and embraced us like we were long lost friends which surprised me. I really didn't remember being in school with some of them. A few of the girls who were really beautiful in high school had put on a lot of weight and looked old beyond their years. Some of the top athletes had huge beer guts hanging over their belts and were decidedly less attractive. There was a lot less hair among the men and most of the women wore glasses and dressed like the middle-aged housewives they were. And then there was Dottie and Eloise, looking as gorgeous as ever. Eloise who had been voted most popular in high school, was married to Chickie who had been voted best dressed. It had taken them a few false starts, but they finally ended up together. The class flirt had married a minister. A couple times, I thought I caught her gazing at one of the former football players, with a come hither look in her eye, but it might have been my imagination. Somehow with the passage of time we had become equals, men and women of a certain age who had shared some wonderful innocent years. Sometime during the evening it dawned on me that we might have been more popular than we realized. As teenagers we had always felt intimidated by the cheerleaders. We had never dared to speak to a football or basketball player, they were so unattainable. But maybe we had been the ones to erect the barriers. A lot of our classmates recalled incidents and shared experiences that in retrospect sounded like we had been pretty well liked.

I had a great time. I reconnected with Richard and found we now had more in common than when we were in high school. Judy Schroeder, who at one time had been a close friend, was not at the reunion but I was able to get her address and phone number. I might just give her a call sometime. Jeanne, who had been a sorority sister, had sadly passed away, which made us all feel very vulnerable.

High school for some of us was the best time in our lives, and for others, it was only the beginning on a long road of hopes and dreams. The bright stars in high school did not all end up being the high achievers, and a few of the no-hopers became quite successful.

I was able to come to grips with some of my own insecurities. I have come to realize that there is a lot more to life than baton twirling and cheerleading. I am pretty sure that no one in our class has built a career around those specific talents, and yet they seemed so important when we were teenagers.

This reunion may be the last one we attend. I hope not, but we are all getting older and drifting farther apart. I think the events of September 11 encouraged some of us to reach out to the past, to try to reconnect to that innocent time when our major worries were a typing test or a date to the dance. For whatever reason, I am glad I went because I learned one very important lesson. I was not the most popular, or the best dressed or even the smartest person in high school, but there is a lot to be said for late bloomers. No one ever had any great expectations for me, so even my meager accomplishments were pretty impressive.

Michele Fishman

The Oncologist's Office

A world exists
where scarves cover
women's heads.

Where emaciated men and women
struggle step by step
to sturdy leather chairs

Nurses in crisp white uniforms
gently insert icy needles
into hands warmed by a human touch.

Those who enter know
the security of scarves,
comfort of white uniformed nurses,
and the fear of a bald head
as strangers look away
without looking at your face.

What Lies Beneath The Reservoir

At 18
after two six packs of beer
you accelerated the car
and drove into the reservoir;
two teens rescued you.

Your mother said it was an accident.

As your wounds healed,
the reservoir continued to lure you
invited you to enter
deep into cold water
where tragic truths are forgiven,
truths that haunt homosexual boys
whose mothers sleep with their sons'
accidents tucked neatly under the pillow.

The Highway

How surprised you must be
to see me drive
down the open highway
without painted lines to confine me

You layered asphalt
with thick white paint
to instill fear in me
a deer blinded by headlights
too frightened to turn

When I veered off
and traveled the road
less taken
you bound my feet
tightly
and sucked the oxygen out

Now I hydroplane and drift
with no headlights
to blind me
no ropes bind my feet

I sink silently
into deep potholes
without calling for you
to pull me out.

The Nursing Home

Fiberglass protects me.
A sign on my tank reminds
those who visit
to treat me with kindness.

I swim in security among sharks who
could devour me in an instant.

Yet down the hall nurses torment
helpless men and women
who can no longer care for
themselves.

If those patients could only become
fish
they would know the security
of the sign above their heads that reminds
people to be kind.

A Mother's Silence

Lace curtains covered a window
where you painted.
Your daughter colored
at the table beside you.

At night, silence was broken.
A station wagon door closed.
Your husband slammed the front door
and shook your easel.

Your daughter hid
locked in her room
clutched her favorite
pink bunny to her chest.

A key turned the lock;
his hands touched her.

Your daughter longed
to turn on the light
and make the monster disappear.

She welcomed daylight
when monsters slept
and little girls dressed
their Barbie Dolls.

Still, you painted.
Water lilies framed the canvas
as cancer ate away your body.

It searched for the dark truths
locked inside you
that you could no longer bear.

It entered your stomach
layer by layer
it destroyed the womb
where you carried your daughter
to ensure that no further children
would leave its security.

After four years of chemotherapy
your fragile hand reached out
pulled open the curtain
you exhaled your final breath.
Water lilies swayed gently in the wind.

How Fickle One Becomes

I spent pointless moments
at a mirror
wrapped strands of hair
set them free
Birds on a spring day.
Now I look in the mirror
a bald head reflects back
How fickle one becomes
Hidden heroes wear wigs in silence.

The Forgotten

Bony, wrinkled hands
clawed fingers like owl talons
hold a faded photograph
witness to another lifetime
when youthful hands
wrapped around her lover's waist.

Eyes glazed, opaque
like fog dusted sidewalks.
Canisters of wisdom
time cannot empty.

A ring of a phone
the youthful sound of
a granddaughter's voice
another excuse
another missed visit
A grandmother's heart sinks
like a capsized boat.

Beyond the telephone receiver
red swollen eyes stare at the phone.

How do we explain the price of swollen eyes
to those too young to listen?

Emma Feix Alberts

Zion National Park

Monoliths of stone
reaching for the heavens
Clouds of white foam
peek coquettishly over the jagged
peaks

Colors change before the eye
red fades to pink as the sun
spreads a loving blanket on the
landscape

Should nature's beauty have a
purpose
or exist only for the eye of the
beholder
what are the colors of the night
when there are no eyes to bear
witness

Emma & Janet

My sister and I are
growing older
We are grandmothers
watching the world anew
through the eyes of
our beloved grandchildren

Sharing our past
mistakes and glories with them
they listen and learn as
we did so long ago at
the feet of our grandparents

We can rely on them to
remember us with kindness
to immortalize us by
sharing our memories with
generations yet to come

The Thread

My tiny newborn fingers held
tightly to the thread
becoming weaker as
the uncontrollable events
of my life unfolded and one day
the thread was gone
I searched to no avail for
the elusive thread
throughout the empty years
of my life

Now in the twilight of my time
I see clearly the thread
attached to the balloon
of my existence floating
into the stratosphere
carrying all my hopes and dreams
as far away as Venus or Mars

How many tugs did it take
To remove the thread from those
tiny unsuspecting fingers

Baby Shoes

In my dream
I gaze lovingly
at mismatched baby shoes

One so small it balances on my finger
the other large enough to fill my hand
Thoughts of past and present converge

The tiny shoe filled
with hope and future
The large shoe filled
with broken dreams

My tears fill them to overflowing

The Poet

When did we make the choice
to share our most intimate feelings
with the world
Why do we open old wounds to
expose the eternal tears or
show the vulnerability in our
quiet times of solitude

Certainly not for monetary gain
nor awards so seldom received
Instead it is a task born to us
to record our
borrowed moment of time
and form an unbroken link
between the past and the future

From the psalms of David to
songs yet to be sung
we the poets must keep the river
of human experience flowing

P.D.

What is the quality of the life of the
Panic Disorder Victim

If I am to judge then I must find
the victim guilty of
no quality at all

Where is the quality in this strange
disorder that steals your last shred
of dignity
that leaves you frozen in fear of
sudden death
unable to fill your lungs
moving backward through a tunnel
away from life

How long can the condition of the
lost life last
I would consider from age three
into middle life
a lifetime
I would also concur that the
prognosis
at worst will continue through
old age
Therefore my conclusion being that
ironically the cure will be the
ultimate fear ... death
How the Gods do enjoy the
Mortal Joke!!

Yvonne Lambert

The Seduction

    It happened in one of those shabby cafes you find off the main street of Northbridge. It had curtains in the windows, placed on each side of the glassed entrance, gray and flyspecked. I had hesitated at the invitation but Mahmed had encouraged me to join him and his good friends in a coffee.
    "Sometime you might see something special there, something you may never see again." He grinned at me, knowing my dislike for anything unusual.
    I was a singularly private man. My life was one of order and neatness. I had ignored the attempts of family and friends to match me up with partners. There was no desire in me to complicate my life with any woman. In any case, there had never been any stirring of the blood or rising of the temperature at the sight of these so-called paragons of beauty or virtue. It wasn't that I was choosy, although I probably am. Perfection was something I strived for in all areas. It was this ridiculous emotion that all assured me I should and would feel one day. Love. I was thirty-five and it hadn't happened yet. I assured myself that it was all a delusion that men created for themselves. I had long ago decided that I would sample the fleeting joys women can bring to a man in the physical sense, without

allowing any simpering emotions to become involved.

As the door opened inwards I felt the humid, smoky air meet my face. Men were seated around laminated tables drinking from those small coffee cups one sees often in Mediterranean restaurants. Some were leaning forward discussing topics intently while there were others resting back against the metal chairs, laughing deeply at some joke. An overhead fan swirled above them ineffectively with only some plastic geraniums stirring their leaves as a sign of its efforts.

I saw her as soon as I sat. My friend had introduced me around the room, and I had shaken hands with a couple of swarthy individuals who were obviously friends of his. Their hands, heavy with the gold rings they wore, hurt my fingers. I rubbed them dubiously as I sat and there she was, curled up in a corner next to a boxed dance floor, her head resting on her hand. Her eyes were closed and her long black hair in uneven greasy strands over her face.

I must have been staring; for the man on my right grinned. He had a gold tooth at the side of his mouth and for a brief second I shivered.

"You like?"

I shook my head and sipped at the thick black liquid my friend had ordered. I made myself look at other things but my mind was on the woman, or was it a child?

He asked me if I liked. My first thought was revulsion. I had been with many women, not all beautiful. But this woman, even at first glance was so unappealing, so ugly that I wanted to leave that place. Yet she drew my eyes again and again.

In God's name why was she there?

The talking carried on around me, but it was soon obvious to them all I was not listening. My friend nudged the man who had spoken before.

"He likes your butterfly."

"No, no, I'm sorry I just wondered about her," I stammered in defense of my rudeness. If she was his woman, I could not say I found her grotesque. But the word butterfly baffled me.

The gold tooth glinted as he spoke again. "She is ugly, yes?" He seemed positively happy at the thought. "And yet she has a gift that draws all men to her. My Butterfly. You must see it later. But for now I will tell you her story." He drew on the cigarette that he held between the middle fingers of his left hand. I felt rather than noticed the other men around us lower their voices to hear the story they must have heard before.

"She is from Sarajevo. He stopped to get my response. That explained the aura of black despair that hung around her. I nodded.

"She is not twenty-two years." Again he stopped. This time I responded openly.

"But she looks..." Again I stammered. He spoke for me.

"Her face has the lines of an old one, a grandmother, no? Yet when I was in Sarajevo five years ago, she had the sweet look of an angel."

Slowly he told me about the terrible life of little Jemelita in the two years of civil war. He spoke of the slaughter, destruction, and devastation that she had witnessed. And finally of the ultimate horror of seeing her family blown to bits in a market square.

"Who knows what else was done to her." Gold tooth shrugged philosophically. "She does not speak of any of it. But we rescued her from one of the camps. I brought her to Australia. She is my niece, my brother's child." She was dismissed with a wave of his hand.

I knew, as did they all, a woman sullied had no value in his culture, whether it was her fault or not. I think I must have begun to love her then, or maybe it was a deep pity that stirred me.

Gold tooth leaned back as if waiting for my question. I was about to ask, but I then noticed a hush had descended over the group. I wondered, maybe they had all been as moved as I. Then the music began to fill the café with its mystical unfamiliar sounds. It was slow at first and I didn't quite know what was happening.

"Ah, my butterfly. She is emerging." His voice was a whisper.

I watched. Fluttering her hands, she began to move in time to the rhythm. The melody was strange and haunting, almost hypnotic. Her head began to turn slowly, swishing her hair so that it caressed her back, her shoulders, and her face. She rose, her legs straightening, her body unfolding, her arms outstretched. Her eyes remained closed. The music became her. She became the music.

We all held our breath. Bewitched. The sweat, the heat, the whirl of the fan melted together in a sensual seduction. She drew us to her in the dance.

Swaying, moving, the colors of the evening swirled before my eyes. My senses reeled. They swelled. I felt the silk of my shirt against my chest. I smelled the coffee as it bubbled in the machine on the counter. The sights, the sounds, the aromas around me were heightened yet my eyes were filled with her.

And I fell in love.

Tammy Stewart

The Symmetry of Eleanor

Eleanor glides on a green swing that sings
with age
anchored to slats of wood by hooks and
fat chains
a hummingbird's miniature nest is
cleverly positioned
helplessly exposed inside a rusty link
five a.m. migration begins
steamy soap smells surge from showered
pores his metal lunch box clangs against a
pitted belt buckle
She is shackled in shame
wishing him dead--- wishing him good day
the stickiness of August in the Steel Valley
crushes Her breath
She lights a cigarette and the smoke
glides down her throat swaying her senses
away from graveyard shifts and fiery furnaces
away from a life embodied by the reek of
sulfur
She shrinks into the salvation of cheap beer
buried under dirty clothes in a tattered
wicker basket
She cleans this place she could not leave,
would not leave
the swing chirps its agonized melody again
but today the pain is physical
it starts deep and low in her chest
cuts into her back like buckshot
sooty clouds explode with heavy rains as

her heart bursts open and robs her rhythm
Suddenly she is an emergency
they rip open her outsides to work on
her insides
yet they can't find the pain
Eleanor hears it--- she hears it
calling
It tells of defeat it whispers weakness
and the pain tells her body it
is time---
time to lie still in a world
not to scale.

Abbreviated

Time rips the boy-mask from my only son's
face
declaring him a man

I slumbered restlessly, but unaware
and awaken now, abbreviated---

From Mommy to Mom, from sage to mute
I ring defenseless, damaged and spent

Time forces me now to wave goodbye
With a hand that once was my mother's

Michael Jemal

In The Strand

In the Strand
I am looking for a poet
who will provoke an afterthought,
a poet who can tell me of the madness
that will not change.
I move up and down these book aisles
disturbed by the voice of metaphor
and the way awkward verbs
taunt me to give up my search.
I am as restless as Lorca in New York
full of depression and in need of duende.
I am reminded of Rimbaud
and his dance on the Breton shore,
how he took beauty on to his lap
and loved her into disappointment.
How Jimenez sits in his mother's garden
amongst his unread poems,
resting in the arms of the immortal.
But I don't think even they will be able
to sustain me through this night.
No, not Neruda with his soft voice
can save me
not Paz who questions his inner eagle
not Verlaine with his sentimental whine
can pacify this inner need,
not even Celan's discarded note book
full of phantom names of hopelessness
can stop what is so apparent.

Tonight I will put my forehead
against as many book spines as I can
and sort through my memories
of the dark years.
How I boiled peyote in salt water
and sipped the earth deep into me,
then awoke in a turquoise house
with a woman who fed me vodka
in a kiss that lasted years.
And when the peyote wore off
she disappeared onto a page
of a book I've yet to read.
Tonight I will walk the streets
in my grandfather's old chesterfield
and look hard for purpose
in the faces of those who pass me.
I will impress in my mind
thoughts of sullenness
in the steps I take towards Clinton Street,
where my mother endured childhood
by washing marble stairs for nickels.
I will search for my voice
in the last shiny token
that will work a turnstile,
in the heavy bellied trash bins,
in the eyes of lovers
that flash like neon
off a cabbies windshield.
I will raise my palms
to a chocking moon and sing to the
inevitability of all things.

Aubade

I give my body to the morning,
impoverished and in need of prayer
as I watch pieces of the sun
inch up the side of the old houses
that have always been old.
I remember her black paint eyes,
her bangs cut high
and the many years it took
for us to sit that one time
on the steps of a neighbor.
I now tell myself
that not her kiss
nor the light that bent from her eyes
could have saved
what I might have dreamt.
To go back to those steps
to sit and listen for my mother
calling me up to dinner,
to watch my father drink his scotch
with the precision of a selfish man,
is to see myself
hungry for the chance
to turn away the old curses
sons so easily assume.
Before the years moved quickly away
from all that was good
on that dark street,
or that beautiful sorrow
in the face of the girl
I left behind.

Sarah Mench

Sonnet

You ask me, daughter, whether love is blind
and wise, a seer like Tiresias
who needs no eyes, whose vision is the mind
that probes beneath the skin's misleading
gloss; or blind drunk, a groping fool,
both stupid and senseless,
swayed by pretty smiles and curves of
youthful bodies, reasons lost amid the flesh,
the only substance it observes.
My dear, confine your knowledge just to this:
it cannot be controlled in whole or part
but governs every sweetly poisonous kiss
and conquers mortal and immortal hearts.
Like wind, it touches yet untouched remains;
all efforts to subdue it are in vain.

Easter Morning

The dead branch breaks off effortlessly
in my hands, revealing green shoots
to the sun and warm April air.
The soil is soft and loamy
without its brittle winter lacquer,
and the pear blossoms yawn
open against the lucent sky.
How plausible resurrection seems
when lavender and mint revive and
the grass bends soundlessly underfoot;
how easy to forget the months of cold,
to deny the inevitable fall.

John Carothers

Stopped In Time

Mississippi had a careless beat during the summer of 1936. There was heat and nostalgia. A good funeral cost two hundred dollars. In the small town of Claggart, in the northwest corner, Jesse Alexander stood in the dust of Sinclair Street. A man of medium stature, parched lips and an oval scar on his forehead, Jesse couldn't read, vote or find a job. He looked up at a large campaign billboard for Franklin Roosevelt. "Gonna deliver me to the Promised Land," Jesse said almost under his breath, "gonna deliver up a brighter day," Jesse didn't see Hiram Alistair walk up beside him. The blow to Jesse's stomach was ferocious. It knocked him clear back to the wooden sidewalk. The blow made him feel like a steam boiler had exploded inside his gut. Jesse had dust in his lungs and a crimson drip at the corner of his mouth. At that moment, a beautiful black Ford pulled in from the street and parked next to Jesse Alexander still lying half on the wooden sidewalk and half in the street.

"How you doing' Hiram?" the owner of the Ford said as he exited his vehicle. It was the warmth of kinsmen. There was the subtle bouquet of timeless familiarity.

"Been doin' good! How you been, Abbott?" Abbott looked down at Jesse. Jesse kept his eyes on the dirt street. Hiram, while turning to leave with Abbott said, "Black boy there was talking 'bout being delivered to the Promised Land. So I delivered him!"

Jesse started to stand and the shattered plates of intestinal agony seemed to be shuffling upwards towards his chest and then to his head. He started moving towards the train station two blocks away. His motions in the hot sun were like a wounded animal dragging itself away from a steel trap. With four dollars in his shoe and his mother gone to her grave in Sedalia, Missouri, Jesse Alexander was going home. He thought of his mother of tiny stature, burlap dresses and the laugh, which always held a slight stutter. Denied everything except an imagination, Jesse's life had been cobbled out of borrowed journeys and long walks at night in the rain where even the stars in heaven seemed to cry.

Jesse walked up to the ticket window at the train station. Poised in his dark blue railroad jacket, pants and tie, Caesar Armstrong stood high on an unseen wooden crate and leaned forward with a slightly frenzied grim. "Imagination," Caesar said softly.

"How much to Sedalia, Missouri?" was Jesse's only response.

Jesse took off his shoe and paid the cost of the ticket, three dollars and fifteen cents. As he turned the corner of the station, he saw a Black family of five standing in the "Negro Waiting Area." Physically, they seemed related to the man in the ticket window and possessed of some strangely mercurial inner direction.

The father spoke directly to Jesse. "I'm Elijah Harper. Where you headed for?"

Jesse said, "Home. Sedalia, Missouri."

Further conversation was halted by the sound of the passenger train pulling into the station.

Elijah said, "We'll talk more 'n the train."

The Black ticket holders all quickly boarded the "Negro Passenger Car," the last car on the train. Locals called it the "Rolling Negro Mansion." It was all peeling red paint and rust stained on the exterior. The seven other passenger cars, reserved for "Whites Only," had a newly painted soft green exterior. In these cars, white children peered lazily out the windows while the adults looked comfortable in their sense of personal security.

The black drapes in the "Negro Passenger Car" were tightly drawn. Jesse Alexander felt almost an intoxication because of the cool air inside the car. He thought, why is the air so cool here? What are they preserving?

"Feels good, don't it?" Elijah was beside him. Elijah spoke gleefully. "The white folks don't have this. Certainly, they have no idea that we have it."

"Why is it so cool?" Jesse asked. "We stored with the meat going to market."

"This is called air conditioning." Elijah continued with a flourish.

Jesse felt a little of his mother's laugh seeping into his soul. That little laugh with the slight stutter.

Elijah then said, "I want you to meet Jacob Hensen. He helped install air conditioning in the Stoneleigh Hotel in Dallas in 1926. He created this system with a pipe here, a vent there, wiring from someplace else. White workers refuse to inspect this car or work on it. It's our railroad."

"Our railroad," Jesse smiled with the sound of the words.

"Yes, our railroad," Elijah raised his right hand as he spoke. "Kind've our Underground Railroad. A train of cool air, kindness, and a feast we share with each other."

As Jesse sat down on an extended couch seat, small elegant Persian rugs were pulled from battered suitcases and placed on the floor. Baskets of food made their luscious appearance. The wife of Elijah Harper then handed Jesse a woven plate with a roast beef sandwich and a small goblet holding chilled cider. The desert began to leave his parched lips and his mind.

Jesse ate, then slowly fell into a deep dream. In his dream, he was visiting a barber who traveled a circuit cutting hair and giving shaves at people's homes. As the dream continued, a customer accused the barber of stealing his fire engine, his goldfish, and his girl. Blows were exchanged between the barber and the customer. Jesse suddenly woke up.

Staring down at Jesse was Elijah and a man not seen on the train before. Elijah, ever the man for introductions said, "This is Crawford Dalton of the West Branch Monarchs. He plays in the Negro Leagues. Crawford is joining the team in Sedalia. He's a pitcher." Crawford Dalton was six feet, five inches tall. A wiry tomahawk of a man who appeared to be in his twenties but his hands had an older quality, almost bordering on decay. Crawford also has a mildly clubbed-right foot.

"Hot Springs, Arkansas," Elijah announced while peering through one of the window drapes. The train began slowing down. In a rapid compression of time and mood, the Persian rugs were secreted back into their suitcases. The woven plates tucked inside handbags. The goblets disappeared under the seats and the coolness left the air.

"One hour layover," Elijah said, "keep track of the time people."

Jesse jumped onto the platform. This was Hot Springs all right. The street was packed with automobiles. The wide boulevard of a street was all heat and flying dust. Every other building was a saloon or a gambling hall. White prostitutes called from windows and lounged against the doors of hotels. Even more slowly, Jesse walked down from the platform steps to the street level. He saw a gangster lean forward and a large revolver, tucked in a shoulder strap, came clearly into view. The man reminded Jesse of his Uncle Warren whose supply of money and bulldog chest was always a comforting memory. With gliding nonchalance, a white girl of fourteen walked directly towards Jesse. She had green eyes and was wearing a soft yellow dress.

"You wantin' or beggin'. I'm for blue pumps and milk shakes. Candy bar be good too. No food in my house and no way to fix the pump out back. It's cool in them woods."

Jesse was hearing the addled voice of his mother at the end. Jesse stepped back slowly towards the train platform and slightly but quickly got back on the Negro Passenger Car. I need to sleep, he thought. Yes, sleep will help - girl could've gotten me killed. Jesse awoke to the sounds of carpentry. Crawford Dalton stood in the mail aisle. It was only Jesse and Crawford on the train. Crawford had built a slender, long coffin of white pine which was mounted on two sawhorses. The coffin lid was laid in place. There was beautiful scrollwork on the wood with two crossed bats. A handsome pitcher's glove was carved into the coffin lid. In the wood were chiseled the words 'Crawford Dalton - Free At Last, Free At Last.'

Where were the others? Where were the others? Jesse could only think with terror. He could hear the train slowing again and saw the sign - Sedalia.

"Don't feel sorry for me," Crawford intoned, "I've lived a good life. Had the best of my mama's sweet tangerine pies. They're gonna draw my coffin out to the cemetery in an old wagon drawn by two mules."

Jesse closed his eyes, and he could see the rain and the stars crying in the heavens.

The train stopped. Crawford left the car quickly, and Jesse followed at a slow pace. A train approached the station from the opposite direction. He saw a white mother and father near the edge of the platform. Their son, a small thin boy with sandy hair, then began running down the platform towards the approaching train. Crawford Dalton bolted past the parents and towards the boy.

The mother screamed, "Stop James Earl! Stop!"

As the boy was about to fall from the platform, Crawford grabbed his right arm and swung him to safety. His action caused Crawford to fall directly backwards onto the track where he was sliced in half by the train.

Jesse stood paralyzed. He remembered nothing further from the day except a man who walked up to the parents saying, "Mr. and Mrs. Ray, is everything all right?"

It was 7:12 in the morning.

Gerri Black

Elvis Applies For Social Security at 67

You'd never expect to see him here
sitting in this dingy office in Atlantic City
on a rainy Monday morning
folded into the metal chair that way:
belly bulging over his pantsuit's wide belt,
frayed collar, soiled white bell bottoms,
ragged cuffs, missing rhinestones.
He is, after all, the King.

But this morning, no more
than a faded icon
nothin' but a hound dog
drawing stares and giggles
from a few curious children
who hover nearby
until he mumbles something like
love me tender
and anxious mothers
call their brood back.

He sits there ---
a refugee from a Fellini film
lit by a garish florescent glow
here in this town of last resorts
where only nights ago
he auditioned for a job
impersonating himself
and once again
out-sequined by youth and vitality.

Memphis, 1949

If, on a summer night, a seeker of beauty and truth
should malinger too long under a certain balcony uptown
where he seeks one last glimpse in vain,
then forgive him (me) these transgressions:
the love of a girl whose family name rings money
and echoes old South dirty politics;
the inscrutable racism that makes skin color and poverty
my only shame, such love for her notwithstanding.

And should the sun appear the following day
dumbly tracing patterns onto the sidewalk,
you'd find me in the Rexall drugstore, downtown,
spirit broken, nursing a Coke,
strains of Miles Davis in the background-
"Straight, No Chaser" at ten in the morning.

The church bells would ring clear across town
and I'd know that up in that room---
the one behind the balcony---
the bride would be pulling on her white dress.
She'd need to leave for the cathedral.
It is her wedding day, you see.
She should have been mine.

Karen M. Peluso

Bed Space After Words

Lying on respective sides
of the bed, they cling to the edge
like cliff-hangers.

Each radiates an aura,
impervious, the way
cement-and-steel barriers

divide highway macadam.
Trapped, like livestock
behind electrified fence,

they lie tensed for the shock
of the slightest touch
or sound of conciliation.

Beyond Boundaries

Compelled, she feels choice less,
like a wood faced marionette
with strings tugged taut.
Yet she picks up one foot

then the other, jerking movements,
involuntary, like gasping for air
when held under water too long.
Home is a lie, a photograph

of holiday smiles, lifeless and flat.
She lives behind the wreathed,
ribbed door--- hides behind
secrets strangling her blue.

She yearns beyond boundaries,
across thresholds, past promises,
moving toward anything
to anywhere but here.

Longing shifts her vision--
forward motion, unsteadily steady,
step by step by step
she walks away.

The Road

I follow manufactured homes on flatbeds,
a southern caravan of cafe curtained
house- halves in the middle lane of I-95.
Their tails proclaim: *We're on our way
to the Show of Homes* --- an annual
celebration.
Salesmen will offer key chains, pens, paper
thin sponges that stretch the promise of
logos: "Forever" and "Lifetime Guarantee."

Lured from highway, I wind past
rural ghosts of trees cloaked in vines,
their cemetery hands clutching life
already spent, through High Springs,
whose billboard points the way:
Turning to God is always a right turn.
South in Gainesville, a bed-sized banner
chants; *Jesus Loves You, Jesus Loves You*

My mind meanders home, seven states north,
a right at Tuckahoe, the seeds planted in
Jersey scrub pine bark, its question carved,
rough-hewn:
     R U SURE U R SAVED?
I think of the doubtless in Georgia, their trios
of white crosses impaling country corner
lawns, remnants of Easter exclaim:
Rejoice! He is risen! as spring's first daffodils
bow their crowned heads.

Suzanne Koiro

Dividing the Assets

I do not want
the kitchen table
you pounded on so hard
it sent dishes crashing
my daughter crying
in her room
fearing what
you would hit next

Take the kitchen table
that held the ruler
you kept
next to your plate
to slap my son's hand
while dinner sat uneaten
on his plate

A Waterfall

A stream wanders through a forest,
cuts ridges
into Mother Earth
races toward the unknown.

Babbles, gurgles
weaves around and over rocks
contains life, sustains life.
Rushes, pulses

Ribbons of white water
powerful and mighty
sparkle, fall, crash
to a tumultuous pool below.

PJ Tighe

Little Boxes

All of the hotdog stands were boarded up with strips of golden planking, sealing in all the mustard, onions, meat odors of the long, joyful summer. It was like nailing summer into a series of coffins.
       —Ray Bradbury, "The Lake"

Little boxes make me comfortable;
I prefer their parameters.
Safety, definition.
They seal hot greasy beach smells into my heart
When autumn is crisp
And life is chilly.

Kindergartners are still flutters in my belly
When little boxes, nailed shut,
Keep them that way.
Husbands are still beaux,
And parents are not in need of my strength
To open jars
And make decisions.

Little boxes imprison me.
Keep me from allowing life to pass.
Yet it does.
Without my permission,
While I cry, "Wait, please, wait,"
And lift dusty lids from dusty boxes on dusty shelves.

I draw thick, deep,
Heady aromas of campfires, twilight bike rides,
Skinned knees, skipped college classes,
Tire swings, wedding vows.
Refusing to exhale,
Knowing I must,
Holding it all in until my body screams for breath.

Another year passes.
"Wait," I whisper again.
"I wasn't ready."

Geoff Rosenberger

The Disorganized Mob

My father always said he was too old for the Army. In his 30's when drafted, he had been running the family bakery business, which he helped start and build during the Great Depression. So, he was used to being in charge and not very good at taking orders, especially from some "young officer candidate flunky that was still wet behind the ears."

He was a foot soldier in a tribe full of Indian chiefs. Everybody seemed to have more stripes, but he always made sure all those chiefs knew and heard his opinion on everything.

A fiercely independent thinker, he was the kind of man who completely dismantled his two seat piper cub airplane before going into the army, so he could hide it, thereby stopping the government from confiscating it for the war effort. He would give it to them if he thought they needed it, but it wasn't theirs to take.

He spoke with great wonderment and hysterical irreverence about the disorganized mob the US Army represented to him. It threw chaos into the orderly life he had already established for himself, and the success he had built for himself against all odds during the Great Depression, without benefit of a formal education.

We don't know the particulars of his army service, his company, or his battalion. He was a Sergeant, a baker and a cook, with a group of men from Pennsylvania, many from around his hometown of Willow Grove, then a rural farm community.

He never talked about the battles he fought or the men who died. He never spoke of guns or tanks or air strikes, except indirectly. In this, he was not an unusual veteran. However, he was unusual in his common sense approach to day-to-day living in the US Army.

He was never quite sure how the Army managed to get him overseas - "just seemed as though he was standing in the wrong line at the wrong time," or how they managed to get him home. Yet, he loved to tell tales about his years there. While the tales told always seemed stretched beyond belief, we have no reason to doubt any of them, because they never seemed to vary with each re-telling.

Dad was known as Hutz everywhere but in the Army. They called him Rosey, a nickname taken from the family name Rosenberger. He had several different jobs during his war years, but primarily he was one of his Battalion's bakers - he cooked for the masses of men, who would wait in endless lines for more food.

(In fact, when first married he gave his bride his army cookbook when she wanted to make biscuits. My mother swore the recipe was for 20,000 biscuits, and he told her to divide).

One story he used to love to tell was about "Army Apple Pie." He had received a truckload of #10 cans that were labeled apples. When he opened the cans, he was surprised to find sauerkraut instead of apples.

He tried to report this finding to his superior, but was told to "pound sand and get out of my office. You don't know what you're talking about. Go make some apple pies." So, he used the sauerkraut to make hundreds of "Army Apple Pies."

The men tried complaining, but he would reply to each "The US Army says it's apples, so it's apples! Now do you want some pie or not? If you got a problem with it - see the lieutenant. He'll tell you it's apples too. That's what he told me!" These "pimply faced kids" weren't going to rile him any more then the Lieutenant.

He, however, continued to do his best to rile those in charge. The pie incident occurred in North Africa, and happened just before he went on "strike." As he describes it, he had marched across just about all of Northern Africa by this point, which he didn't begrudge at all. It was part of being a soldier.

But one day, after setting up camp, which meant the creation of what he called a "humongous" tent city, tanks, trucks, artillery, and thousands of people everywhere, a group was called together and told to go out into the desert and sweep up the footprints. It was supposed to help conceal them from the enemy, and seemed appropriate punishment for the Apple Pie Incident to those in charge.

"What? Are you kidding me? A blind man a hundred miles out can see this camp, and you think if I go out into the desert and start sweeping up the footprints of this hoard, we wouldn't be noticed. You go sweep the desert; I'm staying put." And he sat down and refused to move. He hadn't been much of a union man before this point, but suddenly his idea became infectious. No one wanted to sweep the desert sands anymore than he did.

That kind of common sense and simultaneous disrespect is what continually got him in trouble, but also earned him the respect of his peers. Leading the men in this kind of revolt almost got him court-martialed, but the troops stood behind him, and saw that it did not happened. With or without stripes, he was in charge. Remember, he knew everyone because they all passed through his line daily.

"He's right - What the hell are we sweeping the desert for? - these are the same people that made us eat Sauerkraut Pie."

Even as children we would find ourselves sympathizing with the men as he told this story with such incredulous disbelief in his voice and amazement in his eyes. (Our mother's take on this incident was that by this time he was suffering from Battle Fatigue, a common syndrome among battle weary troops. But, remember, we never heard about the battles he survived.)

As he waltzed you through the war, you eventually found yourself aboard ship crossing the Mediterranean, headed toward the European Theatre. Acting as a cook, his nickname aboard ship - that Crazy Cookie - was firmly entrenched by this point. He always credited the army with originality. At sea for about a month, the ship eventually stopped to pick up more provisions, in Italy.

"I remember Italy. I hated it there."

"When were you there, Pop?"

"During the war."

A load of hotdogs was hoisted on board. It was still tied up with ropes when Dad saw it. He'd been ship bound for a long time, and all they had was canned ham and canned tuna. He hated that stuff and would take a hot dog over a steak any day of the week.

The load of hot dogs was still tied up in the ropes, dangling over the hold, when Dad saw it. He grabbed a large hatchet like a butcher's knife from the galley, climbed to the top of the heap of cartons, and started hacking through the ropes to his personal nirvana.

The Shore Patrol had their rifles trained on him the entire time, or so the story goes. He kept hacking away until he loosened a carton of hot dogs from the ropes. He threw the wooden case over his shoulder, holding it in place with one arm, grabbed the knife with the other, and walked off muttering to the Shore Patrol that they could find him in the galley.

"You can join me, or lock me up, I don't care which!" The smile that stretched across his face showed how pleased he was with his catch of the day. Hot dogs were like mother's milk to him, and I don't think we ever visited Grandmom, his mother, that they weren't served as a side dish at every meal. And yes, the Shore Patrol joined him for hot dogs.

We finally find Dad in Germany, toward the end of the war.

He had grown up speaking German, the son of immigrants. They had family on the other side. His mother, Augusta, had been pelted with stones on the streets of Philadelphia for speaking the Kaiser's language during World War I. It was at that point that my grandfather, Andrew, forbid his family of 11 children to speak German in or out of the house.

"We are Americans now. We speak English, not German." Grandpop and Grandmom had sent four sons to battle in World War II, sacrificing one of them in the Battle of the Bulge - Dad's identical twin brother, Rudy - called Rutz.

As the war wound down, Dad was put in charge of hundreds of POWs that his Battalion had accumulated. Men were all but turning themselves in by this point. They were hungry, dazed, and anxious for the end. Although his German was rusty, it was certainly better than the other GIs.

New on the job, he refused to wear a gun behind the stockade fencing that corralled the prisoners. As a single armed man against hundreds of unarmed men, it would only take a few to jump him, grab the gun, and shoot him dead. Dad reasoned he would never be able to defend himself, and he would much rather be beaten up than killed if trouble erupted.

The more he talked to his "landsmen", the more he yearned to visit his German relatives, many of whom he had met over the years during their visits to America before the war, and all of whom he knew by reputation. This was a war of political leaders, as all wars are, and had never changed his family's love or concern for their cousins still in Germany, and vice versa.

One weekend he decided to go AWOL. He was worried how his family survived the war and wanted to visit them. He made a deal with the leaders of the prisoners and a couple of other GIs that they would watch themselves and cover for him in his absence. And, since none of the POWs wanted to go back to battle, they agreed.

Another enlisted man we knew merely as Lotsy Potsy also had family behind lines and access to a jeep they could "borrow." But, they still needed the appropriate falsified papers to get through certain checkpoints, so a third companion in crime was added to the trip.

Dad would tell the story of pulling up in front of a small building very near his destination in the Frankfurt area. At this point in the story, he would always break into German, interpreting his words along the way.

In front of this building sat two old men, who looked as though they had been sitting there for the entire war. Dad stopped and asked directions to his family's village, Sommerkahl, and after the old men determined they were friends, not foes, a small group seemed to gather round from nowhere.

Dad didn't want to visit his family empty handed, and wanted to bring them some wine. But the old men, and the others who accumulated, assured him they hadn't had wine since shortly after the war started. Not being stupid, and always up to the art of the deal, Dad told them he had something to trade.

"Vas?" the old men asked, suddenly interested.

"Chocolat." A silent hush went over the crowd as you heard them whisper to each other "chocolat...chocolat...chocolat..." He could tell that these people had not tasted "chocolat" in years, due to the war. To make their eyes water as much as their mouths were, he reached behind him into a large box he was bringing his family from the battalion kitchen.

He pulled out some powdered Nestle Cocoa. It was folded into a large sheet of paper, and as the crowd continued to whisper, he unwrapped it before them - much like a diamond merchant would display his wares - a whole pound of this precious commodity. He urged them to taste it.

It was magical to them, no less remarkable than watching a magician pull a rabbit from his empty hat. They hadn't seen chocolate in years and probably hadn't expected to see it for many more to come. Their combined sweet tooth was driving their barely contained desire for this nectar of the gods that the American GI unveiled on the hood of his jeep that day.

Suddenly, and without hesitation, the GIs were ushered into the small building where they found the old men sitting. Inside, they were escorted down into a cellar. Like visiting royalty, they toured underground vault after underground vault, seemingly as large as the Roman Catacombs, and seemingly as old, possibly built by Roman Legions when they wandered this part of the world centuries before.

These rooms were full of casks and bottles of wine as well as other stored treasures. Some bottles were hundreds of years old, and according to Dad the war could have gone on for another twenty years and these people would still not have run out of wine.

Needless to say, Dad and his friends were heroes that day, both to this crowd and in his family's village when he showed up with plenty of chocolate and wine for everyone.

Dad returned to his camp after this extended getaway and rode out the balance of the war uneventfully. He had plenty of pride in what he and his country had done during his tenure with the army, but he never lost his confusion about how the army did it at all.

"It sure wasn't the Officers doing. It was guys, like me, and my buddies, who won the war. I sure do miss some of those guys."

We miss you, too, Dad.

(Sergeant Hubert M. Rosenberger (born February 6, 1912 - died January 1, 2001), was attached to the 23rd General Hospital. He served in Casablanca, Italy, France and Occupied Germany.)

Geoff Rosenberger with memories supplied by John, Geri, Jodi, Debi, Bill and Andrea.

Susanne Kerrigan

A Night At The Ballet

The theater dark.
The black velvet curtain
drawn open,
the moon cast
a stream of silver light
down on the sea.
Beneath the light,
waves of ballerinas
dance across the surface
of the sea.
The curtain closes,
the tides recede.
Ballerinas take
their final bow.

Tearing Down The Walls

Children born
only to bear their ancestors' names
and carry them in their blood.
Their ancestors gone, those who had started
the feud,
not taking it to the grave.

Instilled in the children,
who were soon adding stones to the wall~
Generation after generation
will continue their work
stone on top of stone.
Feuds only build over time.
until we tear down the walls.

Sean Toner

Home of the Brave

You can listen to me now, or follow me later.
 You've seen me before, but you never speak to me. You never have the courage. You talk about me all the time, but you can't look me in the eye. You think that if you ignore me or vote Democrat, you'll make me go away. But I won't. I cant. The chill of the urban night is in my bones, your refuse courses through my veins. I am the Homeless.
 I do not wake in the morning to a radio alarm clock and a comfortable bed. If I'm lucky, if the shelter isn't full, I can sleep on a cot in the corner. But usually I'm in a drain pipe under the off ramp, or in an abandoned car, or on a grate at the base of a thirty story building, heated and empty and lights blazing all night, burning away kilowatt hours of food and clothing and safety.
I'm kicked into consciousness by a police officer, or a car horn, or the siren of an ambulance taking someone-who-can-pay to health. I move. I find a new shadow, or grate, or park bench. Or maybe I eat. I like to root near universities or corporate centers - that's where there's the greatest concentration of trash. I dig through the cans - a half eaten Twinkie, a three day old cheeseburger, the moldy crust of a pizza - a moveable feast for

me. I eat at a dumpster, or a bus stop, or, if I'm lucky and not thrown out, inside the warmth of a Wendys.

After lunch, I dream. I find somewhere to hide, the rail yard, the auto wrecker's, a condemned building. I close my eyes and dream.

I dream of the past - forgotten family, lost friends, missed chances. I dream of the present - of finding discarded clothing that'll fit, or a five laying in the gutter, or an entire McDonald's hamburger that hasn't been touched.

Maybe, if I'm lucky, I go through the day without being jeered at by a busload of kids, or having my cap stolen by another one of my kind, or getting attacked by street teens because it's a lot of fun kicking around throwaways.

No one ever speaks to me. Nobody asks my name. I'm beginning to think my parents should have named me "Get out of the way," because I answer to that every day.

I wish someone would ask me about my life, about my time in Europe, about Pieta in Milan or Monica in Wiesbaden. I've seen the Eiffel Tower, the Leaning Tower, Versailles and the canals of Venice. Then came Vietnam and now I sleep on the gutted remains of a condemned building on the frayed edges of America the Beautiful.

It's been a few weeks since my last shower, three months since my last change of clothing, a year and a half since I last saw the clinic doctor, two years since the last time I heard a Rolling Stones song in its entirety, fifteen since I celebrated Christmas with anything more than a paper plate bent by lukewarm potatoes and stringy turkey on a bench at the Salvation Army.

But I don't mind much because I have something you don't. I have the ability to survive without amenities in the concrete canyons. I know how to turn garbage into dinner, pain into joy, loneliness into company. Recycling is my means of survival.

I don't have to fret about the finish being scratched on my new BMW. Don't have to keep up with the latest styles to fit in at work. Don't have to count calories or watch my cholesterol intake. I have none of your concerns or worries.

I'm telling you about my life because I know a lot about you and you don't know much about me. I put together an awful lot from the scraps you leave around, from conversations overheard as you step around or over me, from shopping lists and memos and love letters I have to dig through to get to my meals. I know your beliefs, your hopes, your dreams. And I know that when you talk about me, you sugar coat the subject the way you do the pollution problem, the drug problem, the crime problem. But you can bet these cavities in civilization won't go away. They'll spread- right up to the door of your warm, safe, suburban home, or your furnished apartment with utilities.

And when they do, you can come and find me and beg me to show you how to dig out a home in the shattered remains of your world. And I won't look you in the eye, and I won't ask you your name. But I will laugh and push you aside and tell you to "Get out of my way."

You can listen to me now, or follow me later.

Family Stew

INGREDIENTS: Diabetes, 2 cases of Alcoholism, Violence, 1 cup of Bankruptcy, Mania and a couple dashes of Depression
1 Man
4 Wives
2 Children, from previous stew
1 Large, tarnished Pot of Modern Sexual Ethics

DIRECTIONS: Place 1 man and 1 wife into pot and mix into homogenous mass. A boy should be produced. Strain boy and add diabetes. Stir back in, adding mania and depression. After five years remove wife. Go ahead and try.

Immediately dump second wife into mixture. Pour in alcohol. A daughter should be produced. Let simmer for seven years, flavoring with mania and diabetes. Remove second wife and daughter. Go ahead and try. See what happens.

Let man and boy sit and stew in depression. For extra spicy flavoring, toss in violence and weapons violations.

Throw in third wife and 2 daughters, twin leftovers from another stew. Do not stir well. Enhance with alcohol and drugs. Fold and add bankruptcy. Remove from heat. Remove wife and 2 daughters. Go ahead and try. See what happens. Taste!

Add colorless fourth wife. Do not flavor with spices. None at all. Keep tepid for the rest of eternity. Go ahead and just try.

YIELD: Should yield 1 to 4 bitter children.

Refrigerate after serving.

D. P. Williams

A Bargain

what would I give up,
... walk away from ...
to never hear any more complaints
any
"you should"
"you never"
"why don't you"
"you ..."
... all of those

they say, you'd die a lonely man...
with no one around
to love you.
and I wonder
what it means, and
what would I give up?

Just The Two of Us

we two...
my son and I ...
are locked in an embattled
embrace,
like two lovers.

why didn't he call...
why won't he return my call...
how did his voice sound last time...
... and next time?

This is painful stuff
and I somewhere,
am still 19, still young
and cannot comprehend
what has happened
and can no longer remember
what my face
looks like.

John Carothers

The Boy From Sandwich Rock

    In 1918, Sandwich Rock was a small village on a stretch of dunes overlooking Narragansett Bay, Rhode Island. Vincent Maraia grew up there with salt in his lungs and the reflection of distant whitecaps in his eyes. In April of 1918, Vincent was a boy of fourteen often mistaken for a man because of his height and mature bearing. He had the odd deep voice of some boys who grow to maturity too quickly. During a warm April afternoon, Vincent took the usual path to a wooded glen just west of the village. The wooded glen rose steadily until it leveled to a natural flat promenade. Ascending to a narrow trail of overhanging limbs and passing the occasional gaping tree frog, he reached the promenade with a panoramic view of Narragansett Bay and several distant villages. Leaning back against one of the Lost Limbs, a curious clump of trees whose branches only grew on one side, Vincent had pleasant, secretive thoughts of Minerva Stone. This little siren of fourteen lived in Sandwich Rock and always had the scent of bayberry on her from the dunes. Yes, she was delicious in her yellow dress. "Crazy too," Vincent said aloud.
    The grip on Vincent's right shoulder was immediate and painful. "Crazy am I," said the voice attached to the gripping hand.

Vincent turned, thrashing in place, and saw the Wizard. Well, that's what they called this hermit who lived in the wooded glen. His actual name was David Arlotte. He looked like a wizard with his long, uncut white hair and his eyebrows which seemed to hang from his skull like fish shavings. He had been a drummer boy with the 20th Rhode Island Regiment in 1864 and lost his right arm during the Battle of the Wilderness in Virginia.

David Arlotte released his grip on Vincent. "Thinkin' the whole thing over. Well, you are, I can tell!" David now assumed the mind reading aspect of a wizard.

"I'm thinkin' about heading back to the village," Vincent replied with progressively less confidence.

The Wizard, now becoming more emphatic stated, "Thinkin' 'bout enlisting. I think you're hearing the drums and the noise like I heard it in 1864. The headlines are an extra size too large, the speech makers ringing and chiming around like Belfry dust. The women also seem a little more excited all the time."

Vincent looked at the sagging empty sleeve on David Arlotte's right side. "We all have our purposes. Mom and Dad gone to their graves. I want to serve my country. This old village will be here when I get back and so will you, Wizard."

Arlotte's cheeks became almost cherubic but the rustling under the Wizard's feet told Vincent that he had gone too far. In a binge of cracking branches and crushed vines, the Wizard chased Vincent from the wooded glen and halfway to Sandwich Rock.

Vincent never looked back. The only glance to the side came when he passed the small Salt Box house where Minerva Stone lived. She was standing in the window in her yellow dress and squeezing her breasts as Vincent continued his flight into the center of town.

Just as Vincent turned the corner of Hazard's General Store, he came flush up against Army Master Sergeant Alfred Taylor. They were only inches apart but Sergeant Taylor said commandingly, "Step right up! How old are you? What's your name?"

"I'm eighteen and my name is Vincent Maraia," came the very confident reply.

Within a matter of hours, with the help of a forged birth certificate and the early maturity which can be a blessing or a curse, Vincent became Private Maraia, United States Army. Following basic training at Fort Miles Standish in Massachusetts, Private Maraia arrived several months later in the Port of Orliere, France. He arrived on a Navy transport, the U.S.S. Finley. It was now August of 1918.

The Port of Orliere was a revelation. Miles of docks were lined with troop transports out of whose hulls poured an unending stream of doughboys. Mammoth cranes wrestled giants crates from the decks of the ships. Large artillery pieces on the docks soaked up the sun like oversized kids on a beach. French women passionately kissed Black Colonial troops from the French colonies. Odd little female beggars held silver dollars on their tongues. The boy of fourteen from Sandwich Rock leaned against a barrel of flour and whistled pleasantly Yankee Doodle Dandy.

"Form up! Form up! Form up!" Shouted a battalion captain. Vincent Maraia was soon on board a troop train headed toward the Western Front. The troop train was sixty cars long - a mix of troop cars and flatbed cars with tanks and artillery pieces strapped in place.

Toward evening, Vincent saw a train of what appeared to be countless passenger cars coming from the opposite direction. But, as the train came whistling by, he knew immediately that this was not a passenger train. Each of the window curtains was drawn shut and there was an American flag at the rear of each compartment. This train was carrying dead soldiers for burial in military cemeteries far from the front.

In the morning, his troop train arrived in Sector E. Sergeant Top McDaniel formed the troops into ranks in the front of the train. They stood silently at attention. Then Vincent heard the sound of another train. But where could this train be coming from? Vincent joined a stunned line of raw troops who also could not believe that a locomotive could be flying through the air. Then with a cyclonic terror that seemed to jam his starched collar right up into his brain, Vincent saw with his eyes that the locomotive in the air was actually a giant incoming shell. Hundreds of men saw death coming straight for them and threw themselves into ditches, craters, through the open flaps of tents, and against any bunched clump of earth that they could find. The shell screamed right over a nearby baseball field and exploded into a nearby army hospital for multiple amputees.

Vincent Maraia, rifle slung tightly over his shoulder, pulled himself up from the mud and began walking, unconsciously, in a swaying Charlie Chaplin style, towards the chow tent. He passed a soldier waiting for chow who said quietly, "Food's okay, it ain't what Grandma used to make but it'll do."

Vincent passed through the end of the chow tent and out through the swinging flaps where he stood at the top of a large shell crater. He looked deeply and quickly into the crater as a sudden burst of lightning illuminated the night sky. Private Vincent Maraia was then flung forward right over the top of the crater by an artillery shell which exploded nearby. When he awoke, it was still night and raining. The force of the blast had shredded his clothes making him appear naked in mud, feces and his own blood. His right leg was riddled with shell fragments and the pain was beyond hell. The whole bottom of the trench was a sink hole of rotting human limbs, floating canteens, and cracked rifles.

Vincent was shocked and sickened at his nakedness. Clawing his way toward the top of the trench, Vincent saw peering down the beautiful face of Minerva Stone. She was ghostly in appearance as bullets passed right through her skull without doing any damage. He heard her voice saying, "Vincent, they threw me out of the Red Cross. Said I lacked morals. Do you think I lack morals?"

Minerva was glorious. She was saintly and degrading at the same time. Vincent pulled himself slowly higher to the top of the trench. The bullets continued to travel through Minerva's skull without effect. She smiled and waved him forward with both hands. "You will protect me, Minerva," Vincent whispered. As Private Maraia lifted himself even with the apparition of her face, the next bullet tore off the top of his skull.

Days later, as an unidentifiable, rotting corpse, his body was place by Army Mortuary Service in a gun metal casket and interred as an "Unknown" at the military cemetery at Orliere, France.

In 1922, the Department of The Army finished the creation of the Tomb of The Unknown Solider at Arlington National Cemetery. From three grave sites in France, three unknown soldiers, including Vincent Maraia, were moved from their sacred burial sites and their bodies brought to a chateau outside Paris. There, a sergeant named Henry Arthur spent the most agonizing hour of his life by himself, finally selecting the casket containing Vincent Maraia as the soldier who would rest in the Tomb of The Unknown Soldier.

On Armistice Day 1922, Private Vincent Maraia, A Soldier Known But To God, was laid to rest in the Tomb of The Unknown Soldier. President Warren Harding spoke of the Unknown Soldier in thoroughly moving and reverential terms. As President Harding left the burial site, he remembered a man, resembling a Wizard leaning against a nearby tree.

Robert E. McCarty

Reality and Beyond

Words such as melanoma
gastroenterology
colorectal surgery held no interest
to me...no concern there
Sickness and death belonged to
others...
remote medical mumbo jumbo

My delusion gives way as reality
quickly strikes home past all
senses
in a fast moving heap of mierda

More foreign vocabulary,
malignancy, chemotherapy,
radiation,
survival statistics, cascades
onto
this new found vulnerability.

White ceiling, white walls, white
sheets
serve to create a surrealistic vision
of passing.
I hear and go on. Finally (for the first time)
I ask myself Where?
Then a sigh and a need not to go on.

To Ponder

To ponder my life as I ponder
the scar
on the inside of my right wrist.
Still, after sixty odd years,
vividly outstanding as the real
pain
of my time on this earth.

As society's PCB's seep
into the hollow recesses and
fissures of our earth's strata,
so into the darkened alleys
of my brain creep poisons of all
the todays and yesterdays.

Screams of the past follow me
down all the Sharpnack Streets
of my life. Memories flow blood red
staining the floor boards of my existence.

Yvonne Lambert

The Celebration

Mavis knew that she would slip away early. She had warned Irma, but of course, she hadn't listened. Mavis signed. It had been that way since Irma had been a young girl. Why, oh why had Harry left her? She shook herself mentally. It was stupid to think of these things now. They were irrelevant.
"Mother" Irma's voice called impatiently from the kitchen, "is your chair near enough the table? We'll want to take the photographs with the cake."

"Yes, yes, I think so," her own voice was weak. Irma didn't hear her.

"Mother! Did you hear me?" The woman came into the room in a flurry, her hands rubbing together, her eyes darting around sharply. She moved over to Mavis' chair and plumped the pillows for the umpteenth time.

"Please don't dear." Mavis said weakly, hating the way her words whined and trembled. She saw a face reflected in the silver teapot beside her. Was that really her face? Was it really her voice? She peered at the backs of her hands. Were these brown, paper thin, wrinkled hands, that lay on her lap, really hers? Her eyes filled and a tear rolled down her contoured cheek. Inside herself she was twenty-two and the world was a place of joy and music and dance. And yet?

And yet here she was, in this place waiting to celebrate. To celebrate what? A life? Gently her mind led her away back to the times of joy.

"Hello." She was shy. Her eyes lowered before his gaze and her friend giggled as she saw her embarrassment.

"Well, I'll leave you both to get acquainted!" She waved and swirled away with her own date. But they didn't have to get to know each other. They knew everything at once. Two minds, two souls, two hearts joined in silence, and she held her hands up to him as he led her to the dance floor. Every detail of that afternoon played itself once more in her heart. And she smiled at their innocence.

"Mother!" Irma's call brought her back to the present.

"Now, Mother, don't drift off; you're going to be interviewed and everything. Oh what a day! There's so much to do. Mother!" Again her voice was sharp. Try to stay awake. Why, this is the most important day of your life."

Important day! Mavis couldn't help it. She was in the bedroom of her old home.

"Now Mavis dear, this is the most important day of your life." It was her father holding her now, his voice shaking with emotion. "I love you so much my dear, be happy."

"Oh Daddy, Daddy, I love you too." She felt the satin against her skin and the breeze from the summerhouse where Harry waited for his bride, whispered joy through her veil.

"I'd better close the window; there's a wind coming up." Her daughter once more intruded busily.

"Now let's see. Have we enough chairs? The whole crowd is coming. Jennifer is bringing the new baby. Oh I do hope it doesn't cry too much. You know mother, I wish it had been a boy, but then Jennifer never did anything to please me, her mother. Isn't it funny how she can't seem to carry a boy, just like you? She is very like you, you know. A dreamer, not a doer."

"It's a boy!" The doctor's face peered at her through the green mask. Harry came in, his face as red as the roses he carried.

Her words to him, "Oh love, it's a boy; it's a boy." She smiled. He nodded; his loving eyes crinkled with worry.

She felt the prick of the needle and heard the thin wail of her son as she drifted off. The roses were still there. Mavis could smell them but they now lay at her feet upon a tiny mound of earth. Harry had his arm around her, and her face was wet with sorrow. She struggled away from it, the sadness, but it pulled at her as much as the joy. She saw the other mound too then, the larger, a little girl's hand in hers. "Don't worry, Mummy, I'll take care of you."

"Oh Harry, oh Harry."

"What's that mother. Did you say something?" Irma settled a plate of sandwiches onto the table. She lovingly smoothed the cloth that had no wrinkles and retreated without listening for a reply. Mavis didn't mind. The room faded again, and she traveled to that other place lightly and wonderingly. Here a schoolroom, a sports field, the picture house, Christmas parties and debutante balls. Irma was there too as a little girl, a young teen, a woman. Mavis saw herself helping, guiding and comforting. There was great happiness, many tears and more sacrifice than one could imagine.

The voices were there also. She could hear all of them, those who had been her companions. They got louder and louder but Irma's voice lifted above the rest.

"A happy birthday to you. Hip Hooray!" Mavis opened her eyes smiling, ready to see her friends. But these were strangers! A flash of light made her flinch and she blinked several times.

"How does it feel Mavis, to be one hundred?

What could she say? The young man who had asked the question would only have been in his twenties.

"She's very happy." Irma answered for her. Mavis lifted her hand in protest but Irma saw it as a gesture of approval. "You see!"

"To what do you attribute your longevity?" The young man asked.

"Well Mother, tell him." Irma answered before Mavis had a chance. "Oh she's had an easy life. I've looked after her since Father died."

Easy life? Mavis left the room again.

"You didn't expect it to be easy did you?" The voice was as cold and dark as the morning in the hospital. Matron led them around the wards, and Mavis wiped the blood from the wounds of the boys from the front. She saw those same boys, battle-scarred and weary, Harry too, trying for non-existent jobs in the thirties. And she fed them soup made from scraps and thistles with moldy bread saved from the hotel garbage. She waved them off once more, and their sons, from the steam clouded station, going to the next war.

And she lived and died with them. She too, suffered with the women who waited.

The voices were all around her again. Their voices this time were the ones she had loved. But she hadn't heard his yet. Mavis knew when she did that she would be happy once more.

"Mother! Mother!" Irma again, shrill and over excited. She got like that often, especially when she was trying too hard.

"Oh, Irma, dear," she longed to say, "sit down and relax." But of course she couldn't. Irma was a martyr to everyone and everything. Mavis would never understand her daughter. Irma saw value in things, money, and status. Mavis knew value was in love. Given and received.

"Do pay attention, the photographer wants to take your picture with the telegramme. It's come Mother, the telegramme from the Queen."

Mavis listened and then she heard it. His voice.

"I've come love, at last."

"Oh Harry, I knew it. I told Irma I'd have to leave early."

"What are you saying mother?" Irma smiled indulgently for the guests. "You can't go. You're not going anywhere. Why it's your birthday."

Mavis smiled at her daughter. "I did warn you my dear."

She breathed deeply. Harry stood before her, taking no notice of the others in the room.

"Come, it's time. No more waiting Mavis, there is to be a celebration."

Mavis shyly looked up at him and held out her hand. "Harry."

He softly swept her away with the summer breeze. A little boy and much joy waited for her. Faintly, behind her, Mavis heard her daughter's voice.

"Mother, you can't do this to me! Mother! It's your birthday!"

Tony Bataglia

Love Poem

We fight like veterans.
Seasoned soldiers
all too familiar
with the chilly passion
of a knife fight
on a stormy day.
bayonets,
blood in our eyes,
the strangulation,
the struggle against clothing
heavy with sweat
and festered vengeance.
The words are bullets.
We both have guns, trenches,
places to hide, survive
until someday, maybe
the conflict dies.

Endangered Species

Our grandfathers,
balding, hawk-nosed
heroic ex-marines.
Gray endangered species
who wield their dignities
against the onslaught
of Alzheimer's disease
Diabetes and Gangrene.

Medical marauders
launch limb-lopping
amputation campaigns
claim victory in the war
against death,
while handicapped heroes
crutch themselves through
pale green halls in open robes
with soiled flaps

Janet A. Feix

Reservations

    As he got into the car and sat next to me, the moonlight reflected on his profile and my heartbeat pronounced a rhythm that could barely contain itself in the confinement of my chest wall. My thoughts simply crashed through, causing my mouth to utter breathlessly, "I love you." My brazen eyes kept his profile in focus while I felt my ears reddening, waiting for the response.
    The only sound was our breathing. If only my mouth could have inhaled the words that were hanging, stranded in that car. Drawing those words from his ears and taking them back to their original hiding place in my heart. I just sat there imagining a large cartoon-like balloon attached to my head with the words "I love you" printed in bold black letters. I stared out of the window as a plane passed overhead and thought I saw the sky filled with puffs of after burn as the plane wrote, "I love you." My eyes watered through a whirlpool of alphabet soup scrambling "I love you" into the remaining eighteen letters as it flushed away. Only seconds had passed since my utterance, and my dry mouth was emptied of any more words.

The silence was broken as the key turned in the ignition and the motor roared its start. I turned to his profile as he said, "We better get going. We've got reservations." I managed a smile, and my head felt as if it nodded. I turned to watch the scenery rush by. I knew we would pretend the words were never spoken, and we would pretend the unspoken words were never heard. We would sit and eat and drink wine and fain interest in our strained and harmless conversation. I would not miss a cue when it was my turn to speak even though the only sound I would hear would be my fork hitting my plate, with the knowledge that this would be the last time I would see him.

The Stranger Within

She danced outside of
and around her life
and whistled other's tune
She learned to tap and even rap
and sometimes she would croon

She bedazzled and razzle dazzled
for so very long
by the final winter of her life
was convinced they played her song

Journey

I had to leave you
fly away...deep inside.
far enough to find the future
to see all I could be...
all I should be.

Then I traveled back
through the jumbled
labyrinth of minutes
through a complex map
of why I could not be.

Now I have returned to... "Now"
only to notice you hadn't noticed
I was gone.

John Carothers

Lonely

Wally Chambers sat looking out the window of his small room. His nose was right up to the glass. It was after midnight and some of the foggy mist had lifted. Wally felt almost as though he could reach out and rub the stars like good luck charms. The occasional beam of light flashing by caused him to turn away. But, just as quickly, his gaze would return to a delicious view of the heavens.

Wally leaned back in his chair and then floated right up to the ceiling. He was weightless and seventy-five million miles from earth. Doing his version of a dolphin roll, Wally curled over several times in mid air before resuming his seat. The mist of cosmic gases was beginning to cloud the window again and those beams of light, small meteors actually were streaking by with greater frequency.

It was the year 2063. One hundred years had passed since the Kennedy assassination. Twenty years had passed since Wally Chambers had last strolled in the Boston Common. Twenty-five years had passed since he'd last had sex. Well, Wally had dwelt on that subject all too often in outer space.

Wally Chambers was a NASA space historian who had 'qualified' for this mission by routinely uncovering discrepancies in NASA records dealing with past space exploration. Not a whistleblower, just a man interested in all sorts of things that routinely, according to his superiors, should have been left undisturbed.

The door opened and in swam, albeit on air, the maintenance man. His name was Joe Bertrand and he had been, in his younger days, a middleweight contender back in Joplin, Missouri. Seventy-five million miles from earth, Joe picked up the trash and separated crew members when arguments got too furious. He had, to Wally's mind, also an almost disturbing sense of keeping things routine.

"Keeping the log, Wally?" Joe asked.

"Oh yeah, I'm right up to the minute on all the aliens we saw today. Even got some interviews that NASA is going to be real impressed with. I mean - it's all first rate stuff." Wally then laughed and added, "they really have visited earth."

Joe Bertrand listened silently. He then forced a somewhat sad laugh while saying, "Isn't it great. The opportunity the government gave us. Really, at this point in our lives, a couple of middle age guys with the chance for peace and quiet."

Wally listened silently. Joe looked back, as though hearing sounds in the corridor. Having finished his rounds, the Maintenance Man snapped his trash pouch shut. Quickly, in good weightless fashion, Joe Bertrand back stroked through mid-air out the door and was gone.

It was more than an opportunity for peace and quiet, Wally thought. There actually was a mission involved. It was the usual, collecting gases and particles with a few DNA experiments thrown in for good measure. Joe Bertrand was okay for an occasional brief conversation, but basically it was like Wally was back at the government desk on earth. Left alone, staring out the window, and often garnering attention only when his curiosity became too pronounced for the general good.

You could assume a lot of things were okay under certain circumstances, Wally pondered while fidgeting in his seat. For a little diversion, Wally had even tried chat room on the Internet. So, with his face again pressed to the glass, he tapped on the window with his left hand while his right hand absently tapped the keyboard on his computer.

Little meteors continued to flash by at a distance. Cosmic gases enveloped them like a froth of a wave following jellyfish. So delicious and soothing in the heavens.

It was then that Wally looked down at the monitor and saw, in flashing yellow against a background of blue, the words - Is that you, Wally?

Wally Chambers stared down in both curiosity and fear for the screen did not contain the usual Origin message nor did it contain any time sent reference.

The message repeated, now in bolder yellow and capitalized print - IS THAT YOU, WALLY?

Wally then hit an over-ride for the dialogue feature and began typing a reply. NASA prohibited dialogue with suspected aliens. Due to lack of origin and time references, this could be an alien. But he was lonely, curious, and not one to always follow the rules.

Yes, it's Wally, and you are?

Not far away.

What is your name? Wally could only ask.

Give me one if that is required, the bold yellow text becoming a more subdued, almost relaxing coral shade.

Wally key stroked in - Charlie.

That's good, just an average name.

Wally, now with the tingling of the uncertain pursuer typed in, You stated you weren't far away. Well how close are you and why are you contacting me?

Wally's thoughts continued to be anxious. He could be fearful sometimes over the smallest things. But, was this really a small thing after all?

ARE YOU STILL THERE, WALLY? - came the print on the screen in searing, bright yellow.

I'M HERE, CHARLIE!

There seemed to be some frustration, some desperation on both sides of the glass, so to speak. It was for a moment like trying to figure out who was the rescuer and who was the victim in a train wreck.

What's the plan, Wally?
The plan, Charlie?
Yes, Wally, I mean - do you want to meet?
Wally Chambers could feel the little ridges of sweat on his forehead. It was the melting effect. He felt uncomfortable with the pursuit yet desperate not to be left alone. My God, what had he typed in? Who or what was this? How close or far away - what had he done?
WALLY! I'm sorry, I didn't mean to shout with the bold letters - came Charlie's further communication.
There seemed to be sincerity there, Wally thought, but again what could happen seventy-five million miles deep in space.
Wally quickly typed in - I'd like to meet but don't know at all who you are or where you're from. Have to think of the rest of the crew. This really would be totally off the books as far as NASA goes.
NASA! The word almost seemed to burn off the monitor as the text coloring passed from bright yellow to flaming orange to undulating, bright red.
Charlie, does the word NASA scare you?
The letter text then faded quickly to soft coral yellow.
I'm sorry, Wally, NASA. It just makes it so exciting!
There seemed to be a soft kittenish quality to the reply. At least it seemed so in Wally's mind as he began to debate further the

possible gender of Charlie. Was it possible that Charlie had a gender - male or female?

Gently, I must pursue this matter, gently. Wally's mind kept turning over the possibilities and dangers of this encounter.

GENTLY? The word appeared in letters that drifted from soft coral yellow to slightly shimmering orange.

My God, this thing - this whatever - can now read my mind. The thought coursed through Wally's skin and left him shaking. Wally looked to the left of his console. There sat his favorite item on board, a giant, old-fashioned glass mason jar. There was a loose collection of pennies at the bottom. Nestled in this little carpet of pennies were several Victorian toy trains and a small sailing ship. It was his 'home away from home.' Wally unstrapped the little metal binder which held it in place on the console. He picked up the Mason jar with both hands and held it just inches from his face.

Wally then saw - indeed almost felt - the dark red gleam beyond the Mason jar. It was like a dark red cloud that seemed to encircle the Mason jar itself. Wally partially lowered the Mason jar from his face. He saw a new message in red letters on the monitor.

IS THAT ALL YOU HAVE TO OFFER ME?

Charlie, Charlie. This is nostalgia. You know? The past! Wally, waited following the keystrokes for a reply.

THE FUTURE! The words again appeared in dark red letters.

Wally then pulled the Mason jar directly back up in front of his face. He held it up like a glass shield - praying that this remnant of the past would provide both psychological and physical protection. Wally drew so close to the glass jar that he began transcending unknown barriers in his mind. A few minutes later - in a capsule of what he sensed was lost time - Wally Chambers was miniaturized to a height of one foot and inside the Mason jar itself.

As he rustled his feet on the carpet of copper pennies, Wally realized the Mason jar was floating in the outside darkness of the heavens.

In the periphery of his sight, letters appeared on the inside of the glass jar. They were dark red and gleaming.

IS THAT YOU WALLY?

Wally Chambers just pressed his nose right up to the glass.

Marion W. Maguire

Silver Bird
Remembering TWA Flight 800

Silver Bird in starry night,
Climbing higher in your flight.
Within your womb, two hundred fold,
Precious loved ones, young and old.

Wounded bird in flames consumed.
Dreams and love in fire doomed.
To the cooling sea now fly,
Swiftly falling from the sky.

Dying bird let ocean spray
Gently wash the flames away.
Soothing, soothing ease the pain,
Of those who wait and hope in vain.

Silent bird in ocean deep,
We must disturb your lonely sleep,
To find what caused this fatal blow.
That you may sleep. That we may know.

Spirit bird fly high, fly free.
In heaven's skies eternally
In our hearts, through pain so raw,
You will live forever more.

Silent Dreams

Sleep, silent dreams,
lest waking
You disturb the leaden complacency
Of my cluttered life.
And open my soul
To awesome vistas
Of wondrous possibilities.

Amanda —

Holly & I hope you enjoy R.J.'s Poems

Love
Rudy & Holly

Editor's Choice

R.J. Corradino wrote, "I don't think writing is about power. I don't feel a desire to create or destroy. My desire is for connections. I write to form connections with people. That's all."

The poetry of R.J. Corradino was selected for the Editor's Choice section of *Winds of Time* because of the connections that the reader makes when reading R.J.'s thought provoking poetry. Throughout the lines of his poetry, R.J. weaves the struggles we endure throughout our life along with life's celebrations. We do indeed connect with the timeless messages portrayed in R.J.'s poetry.

As a student at Richard Stockton College, R.J. studied Literature and Creative Writing under Pulitzer Prize winning poet Stephen Dunn until his untimely death at the age of twenty. Despite his disability and wheelchair dependence, R.J. maintained a loving spirit, a sense of humor, and a quiet dignity. His poetry lives on as a tribute to his memory.

Foreword

Among the many reasons why people loved him was that in his wheelchair, with his physical difficulties, R.J. never attempted to elicit pity. He asked merely to be taken as he was – an interesting young man who shared your interests. I can't say that I loved him (I try not to love my students), but I admired his intelligence, good humor, and most of all his dignity. At the time of his death he was writing, indeed, some very moving poetry. In particular, a love poetry that attested to his imagination as much as it did to his desires.

Though it's doubtful that R.J. had experienced carnal love (I hope he did), he certainly experienced it in his poems. And he also certainly had his dream woman who doubled as his muse; many of his poems are directed to her.

In my favorite poem of his, *"Cancer's Proposal,"* he says,

I am I. I'm nothing more

or less to be

but this body (strange

as it is beautiful, beautiful

as it is amusing)

and proceeds to say to her that, although his

hands are like claws, he has

"eyes...that can embrace you."

Of course, as he's offering her this, he's offering her more: a lovely sensibility, a good mind, a burgeoning talent. That's what he offered us as well.

       Stephen Dunn 2002

R. J. Corradino

Untitled

They say that poets and rock stars must end
with glorious steam and burned fuel,
with a furious halt, like a drunken freight
train.
Such will not be my undoing.
I move on slowly, and I diffuse slowly.

I wake. A day goes. I sleep. I wake.

Each cycle is a small undoing, each day a
choice, each choice a disconnection.
Simply, I will disappear one day (for I have
often wished to do so)
as a wisp of smoke diffused from a powder
puff.

Stephanie's Poem

I wear a silver locket
with a balled up poem inside
that pushes the little door half open,
almost breaks the teeny clasp.
(My boyfriend gave it to me.)
I keep it by my heart,
reminding me
the nicest things we keep inside our hearts
don't always fit exactly.

About a Broken Compass

Such a sad device:
The arrow has pulled
so strongly against the current
that it now spins rather indecisively,
not pointed in any chosen direction.
It's shiny, anyway.

Cancer's Proposal

I'll be your little lobster, if you'd like,
and oh, what a wondrous lover I could be!

I know of men who say they know
true love, but there is a sea that knows
constructed love is not love:
the ocean pulls and tugs at walls
that once had seemed so strong.

I am of that ocean,
and though my body stands
a mile short of man's,
I've felt those earthly waters,
comfortable as sorrow, filled with joy,
they touch the skin
like pillows, moist
with tears and morning dew.

That sea is within us,
yet we did not create it
and it is not for our control.
Be passive. the waves will come
and lick our skin
until they finally draw us in.

Why do you falter
at my offering of passion?
True, I am the thing you see:
strange lobster boy with ragged claws,
clumsy crustacean beast
that adores you.

I remain,
honorably and proudly, subhuman.
I do not speak the word I do not understand.
I am content to feel its power
and let its current guide me.

I am I. I've nothing more
or less to be
but this body (strange
as it is beautiful, beautiful
as it is amusing):

a reddened face,
a shell.
two twisted claws
and two obsidian eyes,
eyes that yearn and deeply care,
that can embrace,
that need you,

eyes that see you
as a radiant mermaid.

Let us, my lady, be wed by the sea.

This is Stillness

as rains seeps
from dim stars,
laughing against
closed windows;

as night wind threatens
door latches;

as a fan whispers
bittersweet, cold silence;

I turn over brittle pages
of this journal
writing nothing

Sunshower

On this sharp, crisp day of spring
we were startled as the first cool splash
of water hit your face
and rolled from your forehead,
down across your nose's bridge,
resting with a smirk beneath your lip.
I kissed it away.

We laughed - running, spinning
as flowers; we enjoyed the feel of joy
infused droplets spinning from our skin,
embracing the brilliant colored fiber
of our clothes, our hair.
In that sunny rain, bathed in liquid color,
you shimmered with the radiance
of the day we met.

Alone in the Kitchen

Her skin parted at the mercy of the broken
wine glass;
His hands and hers.
That is all there is.

Moments as this are rare and crucial.
The party,
the dancers,
the noise fading to a blurry calm,
drifting with the endless moments
leading up to now, to here;
drifting with the vast questions of the future.

She could feel,
touch the moment,
sense it in his fingers,
in his caress,
a clumsy grace
removing the shard from her hand.

Bactine and a Band-aid on her wound,
she dreamily swept the mess
into the dustpan.

On An Outing With My Son

I took him to the park last week
Giving him a coin,
I let him step away from my wheelchair
striding to the pond's edge.
Eyes shut,
face in a knot,
he tossed the silver piece with dignity.

I pulled him to my lap,
hugging him
as tightly as my bony arms could grasp.
We sat together and watched his wish
sink into the murky bottom.
With a dream, a veil
clouding his tiny face,
he told me, "Daddy,
I wish for you to walk some day."

I froze.

I thought of my youth:
Such faith I had in destiny,
God's loving plan
of endless earthly lessons.
I knew,
or used to know
that overcoming a true burden
meant first resigning to it.

Must this be the day I taught my child the art
of giving up?

Confusion, terror filled my heart.
Those wondering eyes
that looked to me
were somehow wiser than my own.

I knew nothing that a father ought to know.
I muttered in my mind a prayer,
thanking God for my son's thoughtfulness
and wishing his faith would linger
longer than my own.

(Untitled)

When we speak,
I want my words to gently
fall against your heart,
letting slip the latches
to your mind

Conversing

So much exchanged:
between two pairs of soft eyes:
the stillness of his body on the bed;
the gentle breeze from her nude form;
in each step of her evening ritual---
hairbrush, shower curtain,
steam, silk nightgown, in her giggle,
in the sock she throws as she
catches him spying yet again;
in his sheepish, blushing smirk.

So many words within: the swish of the top
sheet pulled aside; the rumble of the
mattress as she lays with him, rolling slowly,
her hand crossing over his chest to scratch
his face, resting her chin near his neck,
resting her lips in the space behind his ear,
the kisses, the hisses, the thumps of slow
breaths and heartbeats; the slight crack as
he opens his mouth, words searching for exit;
the single finger, laid upon his lips
the kissing, the gentle nibbling of her hand;
the unspoken redundant word.

Such a pleasant conversation they had,
as they closed their eyes
and drifted, lingering one step above sleep

Super Heroes

Superman is a fraud, just like me.
All we have is what the cosmos gives us.
We deal with our bodies,
however strange they are--
The most we do is cry about it.
In dark rooms, I search in vain for reasons to whine.
I'm no different from the spacy goons and supermen
that walk through time.
Still, some look at me, seeing strength.
They see these weaknesses
and   think I must be somehow stronger than
they believe I look.
"I Guess." I blink.
Each compliment a shaky boulder,
placed upon my boney shoulders.

Overexposure

This photograph makes me breathe a shiver.
My face is gone.
It seems almost a negative,
but negatives are sharp and definite.
Here, I am a blurred streak of white--
a stranger, drenched inside a wash of lights.

Light wraps around me in a coat of fear,
Holding me unsure, as if in darkness

Biographies

Emma Feix Alberts, a native of Philadelphia, Pennsylvania. She now lives in Galloway, New Jersey with her husband, Marty. Emma is known internationally for her book of poetry *All That Is Familiar* and her recent novel *What The Hell Was I Thinking*. Her work has also been featured in the following anthologies, *Cobblestones*, *Traveled Paths* and *Beyond The Seven Bridges*.

Tony Bataglia, wants, *"to be at least as alive as the vulgar ? Frank O'Hara"*. Tony won first prize in the 2001 talent show at *Atlantic Cape Community College* with original poetry and is currently matriculating somewhere in the vortex between *ACCC* and *Stockton College*.

Gerri Black, a teacher of English at *Atlantic Cape Community College*. She loves music, poetry, art and all forms of self-expression. Gerri is currently working on her first novel. She feels that she has learned to appreciate questions more than the answers. Yes, Gerri says, *"Perhaps that most of all..."*

John Carothers, was born in Englewood, New Jersey. He earned a B.A. and a Masters in History at the *University of Connecticut*. He had a career in the Air National Guard in public affairs as an editor and writer. John's work has appeared in *Traveled Paths* and *Beyond The Seven Bridges*. He now resides in Mays Landing, New Jersey with his wife and three children.

Lydia Crompton, is a woman whose achievements include wife and mother, multi-media artist, belly dance instructor, cake designer, calligrapher, corresponding secretary of the *Township of Hamilton Historical Society,* newspaper reporter, picture framer, poet, singer, writer. Her husband, Dave, considers her a true Renaissance woman.

Janet A. Feix, is an award-winning artist whose work has been shown in galleries around the country. Her work graced the covers of *All That Is Familiar, Cobblestones* and *Traveled Paths.* Janet has also been an accomplished writer and poet since her childhood in Philadelphia, Pennsylvania. She now resides in Deptford, New Jersey along with her daughters, Dina and Lisa and her beloved grandchildren Shelby and Ian.

Michele Fishman, holds a master's degree in education and has been a teacher of English and Creative Writing in Southern New Jersey for 13 years. She has been published in four books of poetry, including *Beyond The Seven Bridges.* Michele credits her achievement in poetry to working with BJ Ward, Stephen Dunn and Peter Murphy. She lives with her husband, Drew, whose constant support enables her to live out a writer's dream.

Michael Jemal, has been writing seriously since 1997, taking classes with Stephen

Dunn and B J Ward. His poetry tells stories of interesting and unusual characters. He lives in Ventnor with his wife, Priscilla, and is renowned for his great dinner parties.

Susanne Kerrigan, is an aspiring high school English teacher. She has been writing since childhood. Susanne has been featured in the anthologies, *Traveled Paths* and *Beyond The Seven Bridges*. She has also had articles published by *The Press of Atlantic City, New Jersey*.

Suzanne Koiro, is a Villanova graduate. She is a native of the shore area and has been writing poems since childhood. Her article titled *"Missing"* was published in a church bulletin. She enjoys travel, photography, and sketching, spending time with her family and writing poetry.

Sharon L. Konschak, An artist and writer who enjoys yoga. She is credited with several published works with Certificates of Merit from *The Mad Poets Review* and a winning entry at the *Philadelphia Writer's Conference*. Her short story, Ham and Rye On A Harley, was published in the *National Anthology, Romance Recipes For The Soul*. She has honed her artistic abilities under the tutelage of Stephen Dunn and Peter Murphy.

Judith A. Lambert, is a woman of many accomplishments. She has incorporated her writing into the raising of her children and grandchildren. Judith has been featured in the anthologies, *Traveled Paths, Beyond the Seven Bridges* and has had her lovely stories published in several newspapers.

Yvonne Lambert, was born and raised in London. Her family immigrated to Australia when she was 16. She graduated from *Stotts College* in Perth, Australia with a degree in nursing. When her husband, Aidan, died in 1984 she turned to her writing to help support her family. Yvonne's series of children's stories, *The Groobles*, was performed on Australian radio and became a published work. In 1998 her play, *Dance With A King*, won her the prestigious Kuljak Award.

Robert E. McCarty, is a resident of Cape May, New Jersey. Robert was featured in the anthology *Beyond The Seven Bridges*. He attributes his success to teachers Stephen Dunn and Peter Murphy.

Marion W. Maguire, Began writing in her first years of school. Marion is a Registered Nurse and has been privileged to touch humanity from Africa to America. She has vowed that her writings would always be helpful, healing and hopeful.

Karen M. Peluso, is a fine art photographer from Ocean City, NJ. Her poems and photographs have appeared in *The Journal of NJ Poets, The Potomac Review, Mediphors, Apostrophe* and is forthcoming in *The Connecticut Review, Paterson Literary Review* and *Sow's Ear Poetry Review*. She and her husband writer Clinton B. Campbell spend their winters in Beaufort, South Carolina.

Geoff Rosenberger, Enjoys writing short stories, which capture slices of Americana. In this simple and moving tale of one soldier's fight for survival during complex times, he shares with us his admiration for his father's independent ways and is grateful that the apple didn't fall far from the tree. Geoff is the proud father of Gerard and Anne.

Tammy Stewart, an Ohio Valley native, lives in Mays Landing, NJ with Kenny, her husband, of 25 years. She is the mother of one son, Joshua, a West Point Grad, Army Officer and treasured friend. Tammy's inspiration stems from an enduring need to explore and express through writing the passages of life that can subtly mold new truths.

PJ Tighe, is most interested in writing poetry and short stories with a Christian theme. She lives in Cape May Court House with her husband and five children.

Sean Toner, has won prizes in popular short story, humorous, and personal essay, advanced historical novel and screenplay at the *Philadelphia Writers Conference.* His work is published in *Romance Recipes for the Soul, Beyond the Seven Bridges and New Century Voices.* He lives in Drexel Hill, PA. and Ocean City, N.J.

BJ Ward, is proud to announce that his third book, *Gravedigger's Birthday,* will be released by North Atlantic Books in fall 2002. His work has appeared in *Poetry TriQuarterly, The New York Times, Puerto Del Sol, Long Shot and Poet Lore.* BJ is a poetry instructor at the *New Jersey Governor's School for the Arts.* This summer he joined the resident faculty at The *Frost Place in Franconia, New Hampshire.* He is the recipient of poetry fellowships from the *New Jersey State Council on the Arts,* the *Virginia Center for the Creative Arts,* the *Geraldine R. Dodge Foundation,* the *Alliance for Arts Education* and *Syracuse University,* where he received a M.A. in Creative Writing.

D.P. Williams III, is a member of the faculty at *Arizona State University* in Tempe, Arizona. His work was last published in the anthology *Traveled Paths.*